Parents—you ca[...] your brai[...]

Perfect for home or classroom, *5,001 Things for Kids to Do* will stimulate kids to think, create, and learn. Entertaining and educational, it's the ideal answer to those idle moments in your child's day.

- Plan five vacations you'd like to take
- Find out why dogs walk around in circles before lying down
- Draw a map of a fantasy place
- Learn how to say hello in as many languages as you can
- Become an expert mime
- Write to corporations with ideas for new products
- Make a list of questions you'd like to know the answers to
- Send for a newspaper from the day you were born
- Design your dream room
- Write a story called "if buildings could talk"
- Create a family newspaper

From creating an optical illusion to creating a homemade musical instrument, this imaginative and innovative book will inspire children of all ages.

BARBARA ANN KIPFER, Ph.D., is the author of *14,000 Things to Be Happy About* and *1,400 Things for Kids to Be Happy About*. A mother of two busy boys, she has tried many of the ideas found here in her own home.

5,001
Things for Kids to Do

Barbara Ann Kipfer

CADER BOOKS

A PLUME BOOK

PLUME
Published by the Penguin Group
Penguin Putnam Inc., 375 Hudson Street, New York, New York 10014, U.S.A.
Penguin Books Ltd, 27 Wrights Lane, London W8 5TZ, England
Penguin Books Australia Ltd, Ringwood, Victoria, Australia
Penguin Books Canada Ltd, 10 Alcorn Avenue, Toronto, Ontario, Canada M4V 3B2
Penguin Books (N.Z.) Ltd, 182–190 Wairau Road, Auckland 10, New Zealand

Penguin Books Ltd, Registered Offices: Harmondsworth, Middlesex, England

First published by Plume, a member of Penguin Putnam Inc.

First Printing, March, 2000
10 9 8 7 6 5 4 3 2 1

LIBRARY OF CONGRESS CATALOGING-IN-PUBLICATION DATA:
Kipfer, Barbara Ann.
    5,001 things for kids to do / Barbara Ann Kipfer.
    p. cm.
    ISBN 0-452-28083-4
    1. Creative activities and seat work.   2. Amusements.   I. Title:
Five thousand one things for kids to do   II. Title: Five thousand
and one things for kids to do
    LB1027.25 .K58 2000
    372.5—dc21   99-38434
                                                       CIP

Printed in the United States of America
Set in Remedy Double and Italia
Designed by Julian Hamer

BOOKS ARE AVAILABLE AT QUANTITY DISCOUNTS WHEN USED TO PROMOTE PRODUCTS OR SERVICES.
FOR INFORMATION PLEASE WRITE TO PREMIUM MARKETING DIVISION, PENGUIN PUTNAM INC.,
375 HUDSON STREET, NEW YORK, NEW YORK 10014.

To Keir, Kyle, and Paul

5,001
Things for
Kids to Do

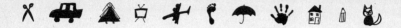

1. Learn CPR
2. Wear an eye patch for a day
3. Design your own logo
4. Write a script
5. Share good news
6. Roller skate/blade in the basement or
   on the driveway
7. Play with somebody else's stuff
8. Make coleslaw from scratch
9. Make a collage from your sticker collection
10. Use a wheel and axle
11. Color by number
12. Treat Mom or Dad to a soda or ice cream
13. Give a compliment
14. Start a recycling project
15. Follow football's preseason

16. Read about underwater exploration and underwater archaeology
17. Do speed walking
18. Learn encyclopedia skills
19. Ask directions
20. Learn to identify rocks and minerals
21. Become a landscape architect
22. Pick a summer camp and write for a brochure
23. Write the lyrics to a song
24. Illustrate your wall calendar
25. Find out why bees buzz
26. Start a discussion group about a special interest
27. Broaden your horizons
28. Name three of Aesop's fables
29. Pretend to be an alien fresh off a spaceship and write a story about it
30. Stop rudeness when you see it
31. Floss your teeth
32. Make a house of cards
33. Solve a math problem
34. Become familiar with state and local governments

5,001 Things for Kids to Do

35. Get to know your teachers
36. Figure out who your animal, plant, and human ancestors were
37. Learn how to identify the classes of snow crystals
38. Reevaluate your clothes for new fashion ideas
39. Read four pages of a dictionary each day
40. Create an adventure at the playground
41. Carry out the theme of a storybook for a day
42. Make your own tickets for a home performance
43. Dangle upside-down
44. Decorate your room for the upcoming holiday
45. Eat pasta al dente
46. Read about the Cold War
47. Be a founding member of an organization
48. Figure out how to use a Roget's thesaurus
49. Plan your recipe for the Pillsbury Bake-Off
50. List all the ice cream flavors you have tried
51. Focus on the positive
52. Attend a gymnastics center
53. Ask questions about the opinions you hear on TV
54. Visit an old-fashioned general store

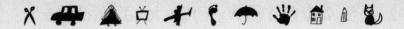

55. Look at things under a microscope
56. Build a dry stone wall
57. Write your first novel—or the plot for it
58. Paint a sidewalk mosaic
59. Try not to step on a crack all day
60. Dream in color
61. Know the smells of new mown hay, sweet fern, mint, and fir
62. Plan a gingerbread house
63. Design your dream room
64. Entertain a visitor
65. Inventory your Happy/Kid Meal toys
66. Choose the lesser of two evils
67. Allow the dust to settle
68. Paint something
69. Learn to slam-dunk
70. Notice daily miracles
71. Make fingerprint pictures with an ink pad
72. Install a night light
73. Learn the language of your ancestors
74. Collect fancy shopping bags

75. Write your diary in secret code
76. Read about teeth
77. Find out why feet swell on airplanes
78. Construct a nature exhibit
79. Listen
80. Start a rock "aquarium"
81. Read a physics textbook
82. Find out why there isn't green grape jelly
83. On the Internet, find out more about your pet or
     having a pet
84. Learn new songs
85. Write down a recipe for trouble
86. Find out why your eyes close when
     you sneeze
87. Sing everything you say for a day
88. Make a pot holder or hot plate pad
89. Learn to listen
90. Walk through puddles in your bare feet
91. Organize a fireside club for a special interest
92. Do your own version of a famous painting
93. Try your hand at writing haiku

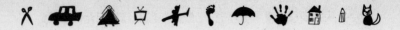

94. Find out why it hurts when you hit your funny bone

95. Plan a garden

96. Draw pictures of Martians

97. Make up a cautionary tale

98. Do everything backward or opposite for the day

99. Volunteer for a beach or park cleanup

100. Read about sculpture

101. Create an objet d'art

102. Embrace the ordinary

103. Perfect your badminton serve

104. Read about the Renaissance

105. Cut out magazine pictures and create a heads and faces collage

106. Write a letter to your descendants

107. Make an airplane instrument panel on a cardboard box

108. Have breakfast in bed

109. Create your own traditions

110. Finish something ahead of time

111. Run

112. Get the pet to sleep with you
113. Read about the voyages of Captain James Cook
114. Finish everything you set out to do
115. Draw something without looking at the paper
116. Know the recommended daily allowances
     and eat them
117. Go to someone's recital
118. Design the computer graphics for a class
     newsletter
119. Give the dog a bath
120. Fix something
121. Plan next year's extracurricular activities
122. Build a piece of furniture
123. Send for an autograph of a famous person
124. Read about sailing and boating
125. Work the phones at a telethon
126. Teach someone younger than you how
     to do something
127. Put your writing arm in a sling for an
     entire afternoon
128. Use onomatopoeia

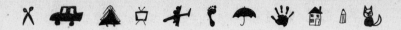

129. Make a pair of bookends
130. Wash the car
131. Teach yourself a new trick
132. Invite a few buddies for pizza and Cokes
133. Do pet-sitting
134. Start a lemonade stand
135. List ten board games based on TV, movies, or books
136. Lie in a hammock
137. Record your fingerprints and footprints with an ink pad
138. Choreograph a performance piece
139. Make a sock toy for a pet
140. Play dress up
141. Compare various authors with other authors
142. Keep a photographic journal
143. Try writing a cinquain
144. Speak more eloquently
145. Feed the squirrels
146. Read a black comedy
147. Do acrostics

5,001 Things for Kids to Do

148. Ask yourself trivia questions from a board game
149. Do a miniature hokeypokey with tiny parts
     of your body
150. Write a "slice of life" story
151. Write down your hopes and dreams
152. Make up songs
153. Find pictures of exotic animals in
     National Geographic
154. Pretend you're spending the day on a yacht
155. Go to bed
156. Write to Nickelodeon to get on *Double Dare*
157. Try to communicate by miming
158. Read about Scotland
159. Practice walking a "tightrope"
160. Learn and use the four-digit extension of
     your zip code
161. Imagine the taste of a banana
162. Read the newspaper
163. Spend an entire day in the library
164. Spend a day alone in the woods, just thinking
165. Read about ships and boats

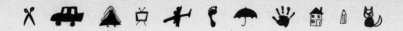

166. Sew a handmade doll
167. Read about Australia
168. Find out what the difference is between partly
     cloudy and partly sunny
169. Solve minor mysteries
170. Pat your head and rub your belly while hopping
     on one foot and singing ABCs
171. Go on a migrating bird watch
172. Write to the Dalai Lama
173. Wear no shoes all day
174. Figure out where your aqueous or vitreous
     humors are
175. Sample foods you have never tried before
176. Hopscotch in the garage or basement
177. Organize your desk
178. Build an Erector set
179. Set up a water slide
180. Wage war against littering
181. Sign up for an advanced course
182. Predict the weather by using the clouds
183. Review a book

184. Swing high on a swing set
185. Use milk cartons to make pint-sized creatures
186. Learn to make pizza
187. Start up a music box
188. Buy a lottery ticket for Mom or Dad
189. Turn the tables
190. Write a note in pictographs
191. Keep a journal of who you are, what you do, what you think and wonder about, and how you feel
192. Read a good storybook
193. Apprentice to somebody
194. Forgive and forget
195. Write a poem
196. Clean your shoe bottoms
197. Invent a secret formula
198. Send out mail so you can get lots of mail back
199. Take a nonworking object apart (one that no one cares if it works again)
200. Gather rock specimens, using a geology hammer
201. Make a suggestion to the mayor
202. Create a clubhouse

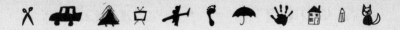

203. Read old *Seventeen* magazines
204. Explore a cave
205. Get to the bottom of something
206. Find out why one side of aluminum foil is shiny
     and the other is dull
207. Make up horoscope predictions for friends
208. Climb tall trees
209. Have a sailboat race in the bathtub
210. Trade stories
211. Eat strictly vegetarian for a day
212. Put together a nature mosaic
213. Rescue an animal in a predicament
214. Write and produce your own "TV show"
215. Make a "Do Not Disturb" door hanger
216. Read about the secret world of caves
217. Read about how textiles and clothing are made
218. Create a cool detective character
219. Write to a faraway friend or relative using
     a word processor
220. Calculate with an abacus
221. Study musical composition

222. Assist a photographer
223. Work with a microscope or telescope
224. Make a classification key for leaves you find
225. Make a tower of disposable drinking cups
226. Square dance
227. Answer the telephone politely
228. Make edible play dough
229. Record yourself singing on tape
230. Name the seven deadly sins
231. Make a mental note
232. Listen to your favorite radio station
233. Plan your own Web page
234. Make a crazy Colorform collage or scene
235. Learn the local history
236. Design the ideal desk
237. Design a botanical garden
238. Create a new board game
239. Paint art deco and art nouveau
240. Clean out your Trapper or ring binder
241. Sing a Gregorian chant
242. Play in a dark room with a cat and a flashlight

243. Take up watercolor painting
244. Test all your pens
245. Be an overachiever
246. Define a problem you want to solve
247. Make a bird-watching life list
248. Go to the florist and watch them make bouquets
    and corsages
249. Stop an argument
250. See how fast you can learn to talk—pick
    something to practice with
251. Help your favorite teacher after school
252. Fix a loose chair or table leg
253. Jump rope double-Dutch style
254. Wade in a cold mountain stream
255. Do jumping jacks
256. Paint a self-portrait
257. Stay up to see the moon rise
258. Apologize to someone for a wrong you may
    have done
259. Try a novelty gag (sneezing powder?) on someone
260. Reorganize a closet

261. Recreate aboriginal art
262. Get into an Indian wrestling match
263. Teach stress management to adults
264. Figure out the cast of the next Hollywood blockbuster
265. Have a backward spelling bee
266. Write a story using obscure, rare words in their correct context
267. Weave a belt from bulky yarn
268. Put on a neighborhood play
269. Use the vacuum cleaner
270. Pretend for a day you're living the life of your favorite TV character
271. Help elderly neighbors with chores
272. Spend a few minutes with a dictionary
273. Read about the Celts
274. Find the toy you recently lost
275. Read about warships
276. Work on a rubber band ball
277. Design a family coat of arms
278. Design a bridge

279. Read this year's Newbery Medal winner
280. Start a fad
281. Paint landscapes
282. Learn to skateboard
283. Clean the doll carriage
284. Share happiness
285. Hone your decision-making skills
286. Put together a traveling art kit
287. Eat more vegetables
288. Practice your musical instrument
289. Practice the piano
290. Learn how to cross the street alone
291. Breakfast by candlelight
292. Select categories and make lists of all the things
     you can think of that fit them
293. Learn to recognize the twenty different kinds
     of marbles
294. Join a public-service organization
295. Start a best-and-worst book of the things that
     happen to you each day
296. Visit a formal garden

5,001 Things for Kids to Do

297. Nap
298. Master "port" and "starboard"
299. Make a sock puppet and let it do all your talking for two hours
300. Fold napkins into swans
301. Learn shorthand
302. Make a suet bell for the birds
303. Teach a pet a new trick
304. Learn fishing safety rules and fishing laws
305. Read about oceans and seas
306. Carry things in a wagon
307. Turn the family into a jug band
308. Play games with your dog or cat
309. Call a parent at work to say "hello" and "I love you"
310. Paint with watercolors
311. Eat wheat germ
312. Baby-sit for an exhausted Mom
313. Take your dog to obedience school
314. Read about quantum mechanics
315. Hold an annual meeting

316. Read the local newspaper
317. Trace the shape of a fossil
318. Wear pajamas all day
319. Make a zooful of animals from egg cartons
320. Draw your favorite toy
321. Count snowflakes
322. Learn how to upholster furniture
323. Make sketches or watercolors of trees
324. Keep in touch with friends from afar
325. Collect postcards
326. Take vocabulary tests
327. Visit "The Legend of Sleepy Hollow" and join in
     Alice's Adventures in Wonderland
328. Read about water
329. Start an artists' colony
330. Train the dog to play Frisbee
331. Learn how to recognize sedimentary,
     metamorphic, and igneous rocks
332. Learn efficient note taking
333. Listen to jazz and blues
334. Give away things you haven't worn in three years

5,001 Things for Kids to Do

335. Make your own birdbath and keep it clean
336. Read between the lines
337. Time holding your breath
338. Write a letter to yourself
339. Make bottle cap art or sculptures
340. Pretend you're doing "color" for a radio
      sports broadcast
341. Count your teeth
342. Read about the Industrial Revolution
343. Look at clothes catalogs
344. Send for tickets to a TV show
345. Talk with the wind
346. Prepare a museum-quality exhibit
347. Take a stroll down memory lane
348. Learn what sports signals mean
349. Discover the best thing since sliced bread
350. Cheat at solitaire
351. Read the 1995 *Diary of Anne Frank*
352. Read the driving rules booklet
353. Figure out which of your feet, legs, arms,
      and ears is bigger

354. Sort socks
355. Create a toy
356. Memorize what metals combine to form what alloys
357. Talk to the animals
358. Master sewing
359. Do handsprings
360. Make up a new card game
361. Start a wish list of things to do in your lifetime
362. Wind up all the wind-up toys
363. Fill up the bathtub and test to see what sinks or floats
364. Put a whoopee cushion in a sneaky place
365. Write a biography of a great person
366. Mark the date when you'll first be eligible to vote
367. Have a confidante
368. Get your grandparents to tell you a juicy story about a parent
369. Draw on a magic slate
370. Give someone a break
371. Think how lucky you are

372. Decorate a box to keep your treasures in
373. Go for a boat ride
374. Pretend you're a restaurant owner
375. Design a piece of storage furniture
376. Understand how the stock market works
377. Make your own board game
378. Read about plate tectonics and
     continental drift
379. Research interesting facts about places you're
     going to visit
380. Submit stories or pictures to a magazine
381. Learn to swim
382. Make friends in another grade
383. Make homemade ice cream
384. Catalog your collections
385. Read about prehistoric life and peoples
386. Dream of acting in your favorite TV show
     or movie
387. Go to Camelot by reading *The Legend
     of King Arthur*
388. Read for thirty minutes

389. Make a list of things you can do and can accomplish this coming summer
390. Put faces on pumpkins
391. Find something orange
392. Study great artists and their works so you can recognize them
393. Read about Martin Luther King Jr.
394. Make scenery for a skit or puppet show
395. Be a science detective
396. Jump rope to "Ring Around the Rosey"
397. Appoint yourself emperor
398. Build a home weather station
399. Retract a lie
400. Build a sand castle
401. Learn self-defense techniques
402. Collect three toys you don't play with anymore and give them to a younger child
403. Take out the garbage without being told
404. Find out why chewing gum and bubble gum are wrapped in different papers
405. Set your hair in curlers

406. Watch an old slapstick movie
407. Teach yourself Chisanbop, a Korean way of calculation using your fingers
408. Keep exotic tropical fish
409. Read about the Normans
410. Commit to a cause you believe in
411. Play wedding
412. Make charcoal sketches
413. Learn to read upside down
414. Make your own personal flag
415. Return all the things you have borrowed
416. Share and share alike
417. Find out why pharmacists stand on raised platforms
418. Draw and paint pets
419. Find out why people didn't smile in old photographs
420. Sing in the shower
421. Spin a gyroscope
422. Keep a calendar record of your moods
423. Time yourself saying the alphabet

424. Do a spring cleanup of the yard
425. Make paper airplane stealth bombers
426. Set aside some books you want to read
427. Have an art contest with recycled materials
428. Take up oil painting
429. Have a make-and-do party
430. Give up on a lost cause
431. Take a mitt and ball to the park
432. Spend the day watching the sun move across the sky
433. Read about evolution
434. Learn a cool "pick a card" trick
435. Carve a potato gargoyle
436. Make a jar terrarium with colored sand, mini shells, topsoil, and watercress seeds
437. Read up on making a ham radio
438. Return a borrowed library book
439. Create homemade party favors
440. Experiment safely with a chemistry set
441. Sled down a hill in the yard
442. Collect old toys and clothes for a yard sale

5,001 Things for Kids to Do

443. Write a letter to convince a government leader to see your side of an issue
444. Read about Japan
445. Be original
446. Pretend you're an elephant
447. Write a great headline
448. Design a coffee table or foot stool
449. Make a facsimile long-lost letter
450. Go fishing
451. Make cocoa with marshmallows
452. Hold a swap meet
453. Cultivate an ant farm
454. Decorate the inside of the birdcage
455. Turn in your read library books
456. Find lost treasure in the bottom of dresser drawers
457. Plan an open house for another cabin or unit at camp
458. Get as many firsthand experiences as possible
459. Find your coccyx
460. Bake a "get well" or "I love you" cake
461. Learn how to take a pulse

462. Snuggle

463. Find pictures to go with every letter of the alphabet and make a collage of them

464. Blow the world's largest gum bubble

465. Paint hearts on your toenails

466. Grow a fruit tree from seed

467. Send a letter to the artist you most admire

468. Change the linens on a bed

469. Be able to name the birds in the yard

470. Make trench candles and waterproof matches

471. Practice your tennis serve and toss

472. List ten kinds of trucks, construction machinery, or farm machinery

473. Make Christmas cards

474. Learn how to take better photographs

475. Write an animal fable

476. Learn dash-and-dot writing

477. Make a portfolio for storing your drawings and paintings

478. Create a compost area in the yard

479. Write a fable with a moral

5,001 Things for Kids to Do

480. Wear shoes that don't match
481. Break a major news story
482. Share your life history with someone
483. Type up the list of books you own
484. Watch a science-fiction movie
485. Fix something for someone
486. Create a rock garden
487. Plan games for a party
488. Make friends with a geek
489. Memorize Lincoln's Gettysburg Address
490. Pretend to be a forest ranger
491. Build a birdhouse
492. Nap in a tree
493. Read about astronomy
494. Learn how to use a slide rule
495. Settle an account
496. Teach the dog to wipe his feet when he comes in from outside
497. Eliminate labels and prejudices in your life
498. Find out when a calf becomes a cow
499. Learn how to make fishing lures

500. Practice your pitching

501. Find your rictus

502. Make an alphabet poster with pictures from
    a magazine

503. Write a postcard to someone you are
    thinking about

504. Think of ten countries you would like to visit

505. Crack a pun

506. Read about the Hapsburgs

507. Read about conquistadors

508. Put on your Sunday best

509. Go through two higher levels in a computer or
    video game

510. Train the dog to obey

511. Have a three-legged race

512. Write down a recipe for friendship

513. Learn to whistle

514. Make a bank shot

515. Design a new and unique bakery item

516. Study cooking

517. Hunt for great rocks, precious stones

518. Stand straight, heels touching a wall,
     and try to bow
519. Learn to express yourself colorfully
     without profanity
520. Make Rorschach ink blots with paper and
     tempera paint
521. Make a stream-of-consciousness list
522. Make a list of twenty-five things that you want to
     experience before you die
523. Be a reporter for a day and write up the news
524. Draw a large apartment building, decorate it, and
     put apartment life in all the windows
525. Dress up like a comic strip character
526. Change your worst personality trait
527. Hang out in the tree house
528. Un-know something that you'd rather not know
529. Measure your room
530. Build a sandcastle with a moat and a canal
531. Find an inclined plane
532. Try making a self-portrait or caricature
533. Develop extraordinary powers of observation

534. Find out why dogs smell funny when wet
535. Make marbelized paper
536. Empty the wastebaskets
537. Offer to go on an outing with an elderly person
538. Silently clear your head
539. Jog someone's memory
540. Make your own finger paints
541. Become the world's most thoughtful friend
542. Polish the silver
543. Plan your bachelor's degree
544. Show movies from a projector
545. Memorize the opening of the Declaration of
       Independence
546. Create a vacant-lot amusement park
547. Take care of a virtual pet
548. Dine by candlelight
549. Find out why chewing gum flavor doesn't last long
550. Find something of every color to match a box of
       sixty-four Crayolas
551. Name the continents in order of size
552. Eat like a horse

553. Take up carving

554. Eat with no hands

555. Bring home the bacon

556. Read about the stages of human growth

557. Call someone who is sick

558. Practice neatness

559. Finger paint

560. Enter sweepstakes

561. Create a new architectural order

562. Learn to snap your fingers

563. Diagram a sentence

564. Rake a big pile of leaves and jump in

565. Grow vegetables you can eat in a salad
     or sandwich

566. Pretend you're living in a palace

567. Become an expert mime

568. Make believe there's a blizzard outside

569. Read about Canada, the second largest country in
     the world

570. Work as an understudy

571. Assemble a family telephone directory

572. Write a citizenship essay
573. Run an ant farm
574. Arrange for a change of scene
575. Sing for a grandparent
576. Write a great love story
577. Think up something really clever for birthday party favors
578. Look for beauty in unexpected places
579. Write a television commercial for your favorite product
580. Write an essay about the abortion issue
581. Send away for free stuff
582. Take a trip back in history—in your imagination
583. Acquire the seven virtues
584. Learn how to pace, walk, trot, and gallop a horse
585. Make a real Mr. Potato Head
586. Learn three clean jokes
587. Study the moon and the stars
588. Rake the carpet
589. Draw a picture with your eyes closed
590. Sculpt Play-Doh

5,001 Things for Kids to Do

591. Observe and imitate
592. Study the Milky Way
593. Look at everyday objects with a new perspective
594. Build a terrarium
595. Exercise your mind
596. Imagine you are on a top-secret adventure
597. Learn a new song on your musical instrument
598. Do the elephant walk, frog leap, and crab walk
599. Bounce a small rubber ball and try to catch it in a funnel
600. Create a pet scrapbook or photo album
601. Borrow a book of scripts from the library
602. Write an account of a basketball game you watched
603. Listen intently
604. Paint a public mural
605. Call your best friend
606. Build a totem pole
607. Clean up your act
608. Make a box for viewing an eclipse
609. Practice a three-point basketball shot

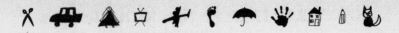

610. Do a crossword puzzle

611. Read about atmosphere

612. List an actor/actress for every letter of the alphabet

613. Find out who is the chief justice of the Supreme Court

614. Pretend you're a scribe

615. Decide how to change a bad habit you have

616. Create a family flag

617. Learn palmistry

618. Blow bubbles

619. Read about the history of Russia

620. Read about Central America's ancient peoples

621. Figure out a magic trick

622. Take spelling quizzes and become unbeatable

623. Build a hideaway in the woods

624. Look for good skipping stones

625. Keep a log of wonders in nature that you experience

626. Organize your pet's medical records, pamphlets, etc.

627. Write down the animals you see in a day

5,001 Things for Kids to Do

628. Design your dream boat
629. Make a twist-tie necklace
630. Explore places you've never been
631. Practice shadow boxing
632. Have a pet show—display stuffed animals
633. Cut out pictures of your favorite actor or actress
634. Write up trivia questions to stump family
     and friends
635. Make real pie crust
636. Make a secret compartment in a drawer
637. Stage a dress rehearsal
638. Master one thing completely
639. Learn a tongue twister
640. Exercise muscles you never knew you had
641. Make a list of as many homonyms as you can
642. Do a blindfold taste test between food or drink
     (Coke, Pepsi)
643. Decorate a coat hanger
644. Make a lapel pin
645. Read about governments
646. Read about Hinduism

647. Think of the single most valuable thing you
     have learned
648. Invent your own similes (clean as a, quiet as a)
649. Practice cheerleading
650. Fix a broken toy for someone
651. Take a photography course
652. Invent a new sport
653. Set the table
654. Practice a firm handshake
655. Collect pond water, tap water, and rain water and
     measure their acidity
656. Describe the typical day in the life of an animal
657. Do Barbie's hair
658. Have a field day
659. Plant a seedling
660. Read the Bill of Rights
661. Plan five vacations you'd like to take, in detail
662. Plant seeds indoors for later outside planting
663. Teach another child to read
664. Do folk, square, or round dancing
665. Write a letter to your future children

5,001 Things for Kids to Do

666. Slide down pine boughs
667. Sing like a rock star
668. Observe a spider spinning its web
669. Grow your own food
670. Get rid of what is no longer useful
671. Read about the Mongol Empire
672. Do strength training
673. Draw an animal that is sleeping
674. Read about spies and espionage
675. Build with original redwood Lincoln Logs
676. Organize a neighborhood or friends'
     Olympic Games
677. Create a new breakfast cereal
678. Learn all the words to your favorite song
679. Find out why geese honk when migrating
680. Make up new endings to familiar stories
681. Make a drawing diary
682. Look for hidden presents
683. Make a salad with five ingredients
684. Make a silly hat
685. Learn how to do semaphore

686. Make maracas with plastic bottles and rice, beans, or macaroni

687. Practice for a dance marathon

688. Learn to sew doll clothes

689. Watch a fly

690. Gather fabric patches to start a quilt

691. "Travel" to another planet

692. Ask Mom or Dad if they need anything from the store

693. Write a story about your grandparents and make it into a present for them

694. Study the rain forest

695. Do something for a special adult

696. Hold an audience

697. Decorate the outside of a can and use it for a collection

698. Stand on your head

699. Design a wedding dress

700. Pick out a favorite flag from among the countries

701. Find a cure for acne

702. Start a patchwork quilt

703. Find out why dogs walk around in circles before lying down
704. Find a shortcut to school
705. Practice your penmanship
706. Write a "letter to the editor"
707. Make a make-believe railroad, airplane, or taxi
708. Go for a run in the woods
709. Enjoy the magic of a Whee-Lo
710. Shampoo your hair
711. Find out why peaches are fuzzy
712. Build a telescope
713. Kick the TV habit
714. Make a parachute out of a handkerchief, string, and clothespin
715. Write an article that you want to develop into a book
716. Write a movie review and hand it out at school
717. Try to outline a story before you start writing it
718. Make someone feel welcome
719. Swim against the tide
720. Learn all the parts of a tree and flower

721. Become a serious student of American history

722. Count the insects you can find in an hour

723. Read about Elizabeth I

724. Help collect used clothing for the homeless

725. Practice making funny faces in the mirror

726. Find your vibrato

727. Do low-impact aerobics

728. Set up a water balloon toss

729. Look for the missing puzzle piece

730. Start a counterculture

731. Practice your ping-pong serve

732. Invent a new and useful home appliance

733. Visit an imaginary planet

734. Make a square knot bracelet

735. Pump up all the sports balls

736. Stage a dance recital

737. Figure out stalagmites and stalactites

738. Read a newspaper and memorize ten facts

739. Make a bird scrapbook of pictures, stories, anecdotes, poems

740. Combine two unrelated machines to make a new one

741. Write down all the good things about yourself
742. Go shunpiking
743. Create interesting tessellations
744. Read about India
745. Smell flowers
746. Find out if every piece of a jigsaw puzzle
    is unique
747. Collect neat advertisements
748. Make up sentences with words that all begin with
    the same letter
749. Decorate stones for paperweights
750. Find a good place to go swimming
751. Do lanyard lacings
752. Write a sitcom based on your friends and family
753. Twirl a baton
754. Wear something your grandparents gave you
755. Read a book about a pet or animal
756. Make a miniature god's-eye
757. Have a paper airplane flying marathon
758. Write down ten things that make you happy
759. Hula hoop

760. Look at everything with a magnifying glass
    for a day
761. Practice one great impression of a celebrity
762. Tie a perfect bow
763. Read aloud to someone
764. Roller skate
765. Do perfect cartwheels
766. Read about the Incas
767. Study flowers and herbs so you recognize them
768. Read about the barbarians of the fourth and
    fifth centuries A.D.
769. Create Christmas cards on the computer
770. Draw a map of a fantasy place
771. Make up a set of goofy house rules
772. Run laps
773. List eight ways to make new friends
774. Put an old plant on the floor in a room with the
    cat and watch what happens
775. Make wax pressings of leaves and flowers
776. Look around a place and try to remember as
    many details as you can

5,001 Things for Kids to Do

777. Make an illustrated list of all the pasta shapes
778. Make a wind chime
779. Knit a scarf
780. Spring-clean the house
781. Discover a star to wish upon
782. Do performance art on a (wide) median strip
783. Make Rice Krispie cheese balls
784. Act in a romantic comedy
785. Look for birds with binoculars
786. Read about Buddhism
787. Write about a fictional love affair
788. Send postcards to friends
789. Challenge yourself with an obstacle course
790. Make a frame for a special gift
791. Paint faces
792. Paint by number
793. Learn to tune-up your bicycle
794. Go a half hour on an exercise bike
795. Read about cameras
796. Author a phrase that becomes a catchword
797. Pretend you are a supermodel

798. Plan a farm
799. Collect materials to build a dog house
800. Read about coal and how it's formed
801. Design a community service project
802. Learn a card trick
803. Dance to "Singin' in the Rain"
804. Learn the art of speech making
805. Draw a great political cartoon
806. Learn dictionary skills
807. Do mental arithmetic
808. Become a good debater
809. Cook a perfect omelet
810. Make a scrapbook
811. Lead a flag ceremony
812. Plan a skit with scenery and costumes
813. Start a science project
814. Write down the birds you see in a day
815. Read about Charlemagne
816. Make a list of questions you'd like to know the answers to
817. Compose a piece of music

818. Do something nice for someone and don't let them know you did it

819. Read about African wildlife

820. Go on a secret mission

821. Really look at what you're seeing

822. Take out the garbage

823. Create a nom de plume

824. Do the Limbo

825. Compare a story about a news event in two or more newspapers

826. Learn how to make a fan-folded napkin

827. Make a kaleidoscope

828. Make lists of everything that flies, rolls, bounces, etc.

829. Find out why dogs have black lips

830. Learn about carbon dating

831. Draw travel "stickers" for all the places you have been

832. Take a long hot shower

833. Study how bicycle gears work

834. Write a proverb from your own experience

835. Time yourself holding your breath
836. Look for dinosaur bones
837. Sew a pot holder from old fabrics
838. Cook a perfect batch of popcorn
839. Learn cool balancing tricks
840. Find out if fish pee
841. Memorize a Shakespeare sonnet
842. Have a talent show with some friends
843. Balance on one or more body parts
844. Read a how-to book about a sport you want
     to learn
845. Find a good place to ride bikes
846. Make an award certificate for someone
847. Write a letter about a law you think needs
     to be changed
848. Make a salad
849. Use your instruction manual to learn to do
     something new on your computer
850. Cut your pet's nails
851. Master the butterfly stroke
852. Find out how a computer works

5,001 Things for Kids to Do

853. Invent a new Häagen-Dazs flavor
854. Study the biggest river in your state
855. Clean your skates
856. Send for the newspaper from the day you were born
857. Have a grassroots jungle safari in a one-square-yard area
858. Make a centerpiece for dinner
859. Read about Ireland
860. Make a poster for a project or meeting
861. Swat flies and bugs
862. Find out about a career you might like to have
863. Study force and motion
864. Make a rag doll
865. Read about knights and heraldry
866. Make a jigsaw puzzle out of a photograph
867. Take your pulse
868. Make the well-being of the land, its plants and animals, vital and sacred
869. Write your name with a whole bunch of crayons at once

870. Read an inaugural address

871. Know what to do and where to go if there's lightning

872. Plan a circuit exercise training system

873. Find out the difference between a lake and a pond

874. Investigate your grandparents' basement or attic for historical documents and artifacts

875. Make a sundial

876. Draw bacteria

877. Draw a picture like M. C. Escher

878. Take all the seeds out of a watermelon

879. Be a waitress/waiter for the next meal

880. Make tie-dye T-shirts

881. Make a list of things taller than you

882. Go to Never-Never Land with "Peter Pan"

883. Write to a cousin

884. Read about Tibet

885. Assemble something

886. See how far you can throw a paper airplane

887. Write a story about a shipboard romance

888. Learn to crochet

5,001 Things for Kids to Do

889. Help clean up a creek or stream
890. Snip six-pack rings
891. Make words of three or more letters from the word *hamster*
892. Create a database for the family tree
893. Make up riddles
894. Play with young children
895. Go on a bird walk in early morning or late evening
896. Make a house out of a giant cardboard box
897. Create and name a new color
898. Walk on stilts
899. Pretend for a day that you live in a tribal village
900. Press flowers into a collage
901. Make a list of scenic vistas in your area
902. At dinnertime, discuss something you've learned
903. Make a design with a paper hole puncher
904. Master *effect* and *affect*
905. Listen to a book on tape
906. Watch neighborhood comings and goings
907. Build a shrine
908. Make frozen fruit kabobs

909. Untangle an impossible knot
910. Trace pictures of animals and then color them
911. Time a traffic light
912. Start a literacy program or volunteer for one
913. Count selected objects passed during a trip
914. Read about habitats, biomes, and ecology
915. Read with someone
916. Practice mental arithmetic
917. Make someone laugh
918. Go watch a trial
919. Sew your own bean bags
920. Listen to a bird's song
921. Recognize shells by their shapes
922. Listen to music from other countries
923. Pretend you are racing at Daytona
924. Write clever poetry for family events
925. Create a snack food sculpture
926. Study the rules for a sport
927. Chart the family tree as far as you can
928. Read about the American Civil War
929. Practice the Golden Rule

5,001 Things for Kids to Do

930. Paint a T-shirt with fabric paint
931. Find a sow bug
932. Make something glow in the dark
933. Make your own business cards
934. Start an environmental club at school
935. Think of things you can time: how long you can hop, how far you can run in a minute, how fast you can thread a needle
936. Write a progressive alphabet story
937. Quote Shakespeare
938. Make a list of the smallest and biggest means of transportation
939. Make a book of favorite quotes
940. Plan a perfect day
941. Make homemade dog biscuits
942. Make a coin purse
943. Make a nose mask of aluminum foil
944. Read about the Russian Revolution
945. List all the appliances in the house
946. Copy everything someone else does
947. Make a leaf bouquet

948. Construct a tent
949. Read about lasers
950. Recite Hamlet's soliloquy
951. Try to read somebody's mind
952. Use old greeting cards to make a collage
953. Pretend you're under house arrest
954. Make up a parlor game
955. Figure out why the chicken crossed the road
956. Do amateur dramatics
957. Make a mask from a paper bag
958. Join a string quartet
959. Create mnemonics
960. Figure out what you would name your
     own airplane
961. Paint a storm scene
962. Create an optical illusion
963. Do shadow drawings
964. Play in the mud
965. Learn the basic food groups and food pyramid
966. Make edible jewelry of mini pretzels, cereals,
     candies with holes, and thin strands of licorice

5,001 Things for Kids to Do

967. Read ten pages of a novel
968. Find out why barns are red
969. Join a jogging club
970. Barter for something you want
971. Read about trucks
972. Read four encyclopedia articles a day
973. Observe a living thing for fifteen minutes
974. Take a walk around the block
975. Keep inspirational books by the bed
976. Open a bank account
977. Apply for a passport
978. Put together a gourmet picnic
979. Find out why $ is the symbol for a U.S. dollar
980. Come up with seven considerate things to do for your sister or brother
981. Interview a parent about their childhood
982. Dedicate a song to someone over the radio
983. Find a great pizza recipe
984. Invent underwear that doesn't wedgie
985. Gather items in a shoe box as a CARE package
986. Toss a grape and catch it in your mouth

987. Apply découpage to a book
988. Invent goofy songs
989. Tape a picture to the window, tape paper over it, and trace the picture
990. Make a list of things that stretch
991. Find out why pistachio ice cream is colored green
992. Do creative crayoning
993. Paint a landscape
994. Find out how marshmallows were invented
995. Get up early to watch the sun rise
996. Bring Mom something to drink
997. Think of something likable about someone you dislike
998. Make up a song about your family
999. Plan Mother's Day and Father's Day gifts
1000. Clip pictures out of newspapers or magazines and write funny captions for them
1001. Seek out a secret hideaway
1002. Search for meteorites
1003. Learn to convert Fahrenheit to Celsius
1004. Inflate a beach ball

1005. Read about the moon

1006. Use a tape recorder to interview your
oldest relatives

1007. Look for ghosts

1008. Tell a story in three steps by drawing
three cartoons

1009. Blow-dry your hair

1010. Visit Narnia, created by C. S. Lewis

1011. Memorize the periodic table of the elements

1012. Start a smile file of jokes, articles, and cartoons
that make you laugh

1013. Create a flip book with index cards

1014. Put together a survival kit

1015. Learn to identify the music of Chopin, Mozart,
and Beethoven

1016. Hide things

1017. Read about radar

1018. Dowse for water

1019. Find out why fingernails grow faster than toenails

1020. Make napkin rings

1021. Invent a new food combination

X 🚗 ⛺ 📺 ✈ 👣 ☂ 🖐 🏠 ✏ 🐈

1022. Figure out how to make a million dollars

1023. Do a splatter print

1024. Check all the expiration dates

1025. Send for a map from every state you have visited

1026. Visit Lilliput by reading *Gulliver's Travels*

1027. Imitate everyday sounds

1028. Have a family weigh-in

1029. Find out why cats don't like to swim

1030. Plan how to earn the Nobel Peace Prize

1031. Start a trendy new "generation"

1032. Make a three-bean salad

1033. Sleep in a hammock

1034. Sit in a lawn chair under the sprinkler

1035. Have a bike wash

1036. Plant herbs from seeds in a window box

1037. Circulate a petition

1038. Make a wastebasket

1039. List show-and-tell items you'd like to present

1040. Write up "twenty-five uses for leftover
        mashed potatoes"

1041. Read about Israel

5,001 Things for Kids to Do

1042. Learn to whistle with two fingers

1043. Make place mats for the next family meal

1044. Build an imaginative construction out
of different boxes

1045. Read about plastics

1046. Write a classified ad to sell something

1047. Make a non-toxic cleaner with baking soda and
water, vinegar and water

1048. Find out what your first, middle, and last name
mean and what language they came from

1049. Draw a chalk town on the driveway

1050. Make frozen bananacicles

1051. Reorganize your desk

1052. Create a marble raceway

1053. Throw a Frisbee straight

1054. Learn weights and measures

1055. Go to an animal preserve

1056. Create an amusement park in the backyard

1057. Shoot marbles

1058. Bury treasure and make a map for it

1059. Read about the Iron Age

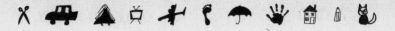

1060. Keep an ongoing record of rainfall with a rain gauge

1061. Make stone "sculptures"

1062. Gain a new ability

1063. Figure out where your limbic system is

1064. Read about the huge library at Alexandria

1065. Learn how to write Chinese numerals

1066. Read the *American Red Cross First Aid and Safety Handbook*

1067. Have a really honest conversation with your parents

1068. Make a list as long as your arm

1069. Create an in-home concert

1070. Grow a plant indoors

1071. Have a peanut race

1072. Learn to twirl and toss a baton

1073. Ride a bike

1074. Make a Maypole

1075. Find a liquid turning to a solid

1076. Design a tablecloth

1077. Read your parents a bedtime story

1078. Keep a record of the good things that happen each day

1079. Collect Barbie dolls for fun and profit

1080. Try for a solo for the upcoming concert

1081. Do informal dramatics

1082. Predict Oscar/Emmy winners

1083. Create a coupon booklet of special favors as a gift for someone

1084. Dream big dreams

1085. Read about World War II

1086. Read about different types of energy and electricity

1087. Look up the word *anagram*

1088. Check out a costume-making book from the library

1089. Memorize *The Night Before Christmas*

1090. Pick a pet name

1091. Learn to recognize poisonous and edible mushrooms

1092. Create Christmas or Chanukah stockings

1093. Experiment with new clothes ideas and combinations

1094. Conquer a fear
1095. Find an oasis
1096. Learn to recognize fossils
1097. Write a story called "if buildings could talk"
1098. Set up your electric train
1099. Produce and perform a play from the past
1100. Learn to shuffle and cut
1101. Make popsicles
1102. Choose a papier mâché project
1103. Master the yo-yo
1104. Make a family newspaper
1105. Throw a boomerang
1106. Read about deserts
1107. Grow a pineapple plant
1108. Make lunch for your brother or sister
1109. See a vast night sky throbbing with stars
1110. Serve "tea"
1111. Camp out under the dining room table
1112. Learn football plays
1113. Glue corks together to make a sculpture
1114. Read about the wheel

1115. Spend a day blindfolded

1116. Create a conundrum

1117. Do a hundred push-ups

1118. Organize a team to play a game

1119. List your favorite foods

1120. Put together a traveling mail kit

1121. Call the White House

1122. Rearrange the pictures and knickknacks in your room

1123. Stage a circus

1124. Set up an obstacle course

1125. Go through the marker supply, testing for dried-up ones

1126. Write a poem as a gift

1127. Build a model sailboat that sails

1128. Adopt a foster child in another country

1129. Read about storms

1130. Pretend to be a master of ceremonies

1131. Become an expert at using a calculator

1132. Be a mentor

1133. Read about France

1134. Take a day trip to an arboretum

1135. Become an inventor

1136. Prepare a treasure hunt as a birthday gift
for someone

1137. Learn to recognize different trees by their leaves
and needles

1138. Help Grandma bake

1139. Find the lyrics for a song you like

1140. Do everything with your non-favored hand

1141. Give yourself a pedicure

1142. Write down all the weird things you've
wondered about

1143. Write up a parent report card

1144. Build a better mouse trap

1145. Read the computer's manual

1146. Have a clean-up or painting day

1147. Build a scarecrow

1148. Learn signing

1149. Bring someone a present

1150. Study industrial archaeology

1151. Plan a haunted house

1152. Find out why some watermelon seeds are
white and some black

1153. Trampoline

1154. Walk a dog for a sick neighbor

1155. Learn how to read a magnetic compass

1156. Learn something new every day

1157. Read about the Bronze Age

1158. Pretend you are living in the Bronze Age
for a day

1159. Look up the probability of winning the grand prize
in the state lottery or a national contest

1160. Find a sport you enjoy

1161. Participate in Chinese New Year

1162. Pick a college to root for

1163. Discover a comet

1164. Call to reserve a special video at the video store

1165. Make a teeny tiny house out of toothpicks

1166. See how high you can jump

1167. Find an uplifting message and write it down

1168. Rent a movie

1169. Find out why dinner plates are round

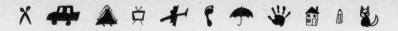

1170. Make a best- and worst-dressed list
        for your friends
1171. Read a story to someone who cannot read
1172. Run a hundred yards
1173. Help a sibling with a school subject
1174. Invent a squirrel-proof bird feeder
1175. Make a finger ring out of a dollar bill
1176. Teach English to a foreigner
1177. Sing your school song
1178. Put the Christmas card/gift list on computer
1179. Read about air
1180. Decide what you would do if you were invisible
        for a day
1181. Set up a raffle
1182. Pick up litter and put it where it belongs
1183. Visit a recreation center
1184. Swim
1185. Furnish your room with unique pillows
1186. List all the sounds you can detect
1187. Bring some cookies or a plant cutting to
        an elderly neighbor

5,001 Things for Kids to Do

1188. Pick a topic and study it in depth

1189. Read about dinosaurs

1190. Listen to a story/book on tape

1191. Beat a record

1192. Find out why athletic shoelaces are so long

1193. Write down the people you see in a day

1194. Read to your brother or sister

1195. Find out how aspirin finds a headache

1196. Collect the stamps of foreign nations

1197. Remove the inside of an egg by blowing

1198. Research the history of the neighborhood

1199. Find out why telephone keypads are arranged
differently from calculator keypads

1200. Watch a best friend's game or practice

1201. Make custom luggage tags

1202. Read about the history of card playing

1203. Bake cookies or brownies

1204. Make a collage from seeds

1205. Hunt for fossils

1206. Learn to do a basting stitch, running stitch, and
blanket stitch

1207. Balance a tipped saltshaker in salt

1208. Work on earning a merit badge in scouting

1209. Be ball girl/boy at the courts or baseball field

1210. Read about the Statue of Liberty's story

1211. Play the bottle flute

1212. Play with clay

1213. Decorate a brick for a doorstop

1214. Write a sequel to your favorite movie

1215. Design a corporate logo

1216. Find out why tennis balls are fuzzy

1217. Find out why there is a warning label on mattresses

1218. Look at microscopic life

1219. Browse a multi-volume dictionary or encyclopedia

1220. Join a gymnastics group

1221. Solve Myst and Riven

1222. Know how to change a tire

1223. Be the butler or maid for the day

1224. Plan a back-to-school party

1225. Clean out your drawers (and closet)

1226. Flip a coin and keep track of the number of heads and tails

1227. Make real peanut butter

1228. Try tracing your roots by consulting books on genealogy

1229. Learn the difference between a food chain and food web

1230. Make a dinosaur-shaped sandwich

1231. Build a robot

1232. Teach yourself fashion design

1233. Net insects

1234. Do the hokeypokey

1235. Teach a cat to fetch

1236. Flip the mattress on your bed (once a year)

1237. Race

1238. Put the family photos away in a photo album

1239. Imagine you are the main character in a book you have read and figure out what you would have done differently

1240. Assemble a portfolio of your art for a show

1241. Learn to do something in a better or more efficient way

1242. Spend five days focusing on your five senses— one day per sense

1243. Build a town out of Lego blocks
1244. Make sponge paintings with tempera or
        poster paints
1245. Master the Internet
1246. Use every Lego you have to build something
1247. Start a fan club
1248. Make a sock puppet
1249. Pretend you're a foreign correspondent
1250. Make a toy for the cat or dog
1251. Perfect a magic trick
1252. Have a cannonball contest at a pool
1253. Compile your own version of sixty-four Crayolas
1254. Learn how a car works
1255. Write a letter to the newspaper about a
        community problem
1256. Whittle a toy
1257. Find out why the Netherlands is also Holland
1258. Study space flight
1259. Read about the Great Depression
1260. Celebrate an achievement
1261. Do karaoke

1262. Arrange to go to the beach or pool

1263. Pretend you're cruising the fjords of Norway

1264. Write a town song

1265. Collect magazine covers that might be worth
      something someday

1266. On the computer, make lists of trivia
      you know

1267. Write a book that will change people's lives

1268. Paint a picket fence

1269. Read about ancient Greece

1270. Gain some exposure to great works of art

1271. Build a stone wall

1272. Do grocery shopping for someone

1273. Plan your next birthday party

1274. Play with a Wooly Willy

1275. Study Greek mythology

1276. Learn about root words and their meanings

1277. Make a flip book

1278. Produce a documentary for public television

1279. Read about magnetism

1280. Whittle or carve objects

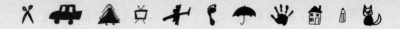

1281. Create a list of stumper questions that only you know the answers to

1282. Read about volcanoes

1283. Stage a beauty pageant

1284. Play with MicroMachines

1285. Build a model airplane

1286. Start a baby-sitting service

1287. Tie an unbreakable knot

1288. Wear red toenail polish

1289. Learn what a route card is used for and how to make one

1290. Start a garden from scratch

1291. Carve soap sculptures

1292. Make marionettes

1293. Paint and make designs by blowing it with a straw

1294. Make a list of things to take to the moon

1295. Make a list of things that can break

1296. Learn how to dance the watusi

1297. Crack open a brand-new deck of cards

1298. Find out why there are cracks on sidewalks at regular intervals

5,001 Things for Kids to Do

1299. Keep a diary of important events in your life
1300. Make a freehand sketch
1301. Play a symphony by Haydn
1302. Pick up a carton of milk at the grocery store
1303. Make your own play dough
1304. Design a miniature golf course with soup or juice cans
1305. Illustrate your favorite story
1306. Identify birds in the backyard using a guide or encyclopedia
1307. Play beat-the-clock as you get ready for school or an activity
1308. Make your own snow dome with crushed egg shells for "snow"
1309. Sweep out the garage
1310. Read about the Middle Ages
1311. Read about mountains
1312. Listen to a police radio band
1313. Check out an old town hall or other historic building
1314. Master a pogo stick

1315. Make a tissue paper "stained-glass" window

1316. Draw things that go bump in the night

1317. Concoct a secret formula for a line of cosmetics

1318. Investigate why bubbles are round

1319. Draw Camelot

1320. Study an ancient culture

1321. Put rock specimens in boxes with cardboard
        compartments

1322. Invent a holiday

1323. Make your own ID card

1324. Dam up a creek

1325. Trace from a comic book

1326. Wear a gardenia

1327. Whistle on a blade of grass

1328. Make pleat-and-dye prints with paper towels
        and food coloring

1329. Batik a white T-shirt

1330. Learn your great-grandparents' names and what
        they did

1331. Set up a game of musical chairs

1332. Make your own costume

1333. Have a camp-out in the basement or backyard
1334. Do crayon rubbings of items with different textures
1335. Play "Happy Birthday" on a push-button phone for someone
1336. Do an aerobic activity for thirty minutes
1337. List a hundred good things that have happened in your life
1338. Write your autobiography
1339. Set up a sticker factory, making one-of-a-kind stickers to add to your collection
1340. Read the history of the Jews and Judaism
1341. Do an elaborate pretend game
1342. Collect the works of Charles Schulz
1343. Chase lightning bugs
1344. Spin a dreidel
1345. Make a cootie-catcher/fortune-teller
1346. Make a picture from fallen leaves
1347. Read *Charlotte's Web*
1348. Have a Mardi Gras celebration
1349. Wear a sandwich board
1350. Check all the things you own that run on batteries

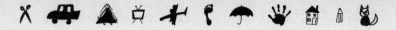

1351. Jog fifteen minutes to music

1352. Think of five ways to cure hiccups

1353. Make marshmallow monsters or snowmen

1354. Do Colorforms

1355. Stack building blocks or alphabet blocks as high as they will go

1356. Learn lunch counter lingo

1357. Start a nature notebook or field guide to the local area

1358. Make snow angels

1359. Decide on a vanity license plate

1360. Learn basket weaving

1361. Sell your crafts at a craft fair

1362. Make food in an Easy Bake oven

1363. Make gak

1364. Write your own crossword puzzle with clues

1365. Learn to paddle a canoe

1366. Help plan a picnic or family outing

1367. Draw pictures of animals that are creature combinations

1368. Figure out the single most valuable thing you've learned

5,001 Things for Kids to Do

1369. Learn to draw something difficult by tracing

1370. Plan a birthday pajama party

1371. Read about the Roman empire

1372. Find a treasure in the attic

1373. Read Thoreau's *Walden*

1374. Make a wind chime from old metal junk

1375. Solve a book of brain teasers

1376. Mend a piece of your own clothing

1377. Take a bubble bath

1378. Do peer counseling

1379. Create a detective character

1380. Feed a stranger's expired parking meter

1381. Read about Pompeii

1382. Draw abstract designs without lifting the pen off the paper

1383. Count out-of-state license plates

1384. Create a paper chain for the Christmas tree or a birthday party

1385. Dedicate a song on the radio

1386. Read about dams

1387. Make candleholders

1388. Inventory the house

1389. Throw confetti

1390. Write captions for the family photographs

1391. Learn outdoor living skills

1392. Make a home movie of your pet

1393. Send a lot of Valentine cards

1394. Spend time with the family pets

1395. Study seeds and their dispersal

1396. Shoot a few hoops

1397. Listen to recorded music

1398. Perfect your batting stance

1399. Send a chain letter

1400. Pick a favorite saying

1401. Take up one of the martial arts; check into lessons

1402. Make a jigsaw puzzle for someone

1403. Go ten-for-ten from the free-throw line

1404. Find something that's lost with detective work

1405. Put your artwork on the refrigerator

1406. Try to fold a piece of paper in half more than
      seven times

1407. Do a sack race

5,001 Things for Kids to Do

1408. Stage a quiz show

1409. Listen to zydeco music

1410. Trace around objects on paper

1411. Try to remember what color eyes your three best
      friends have

1412. Make your own pickles

1413. Hit the bull's-eye on a dartboard

1414. Make pom-pom pipe cleaner creatures

1415. Read about a sport's beginning

1416. Learn hand bookbinding

1417. Mix juices to make a new flavor

1418. Break dance

1419. Go a week without eating junk food

1420. Make a place for everything and keep everything
      in its place

1421. Start a book of original clothing designs

1422. Pretend you're driving a Ferrari

1423. Try to catch foul balls at a baseball game

1424. Name the five food groups

1425. Leave flowers on a neighbor's doorstep

1426. Find out your latitude and longitude

1427. Practice the "Star-Spangled Banner"
1428. Figure out the rule for adding -*able* or -*ible* to the end of a word
1429. Make a funniest home video
1430. Learn to float
1431. Learn the origin of your state's name
1432. Keep a weather chart using international weather symbols
1433. Seesaw
1434. Learn the difference between types of bridges
1435. Read about satellites
1436. Read about the brain
1437. Use different objects as stencils
1438. Study botany
1439. Visit a park
1440. Build a tree house
1441. Touch your tongue to your nose
1442. Wear socks that don't match
1443. Weave a flower necklace
1444. Hunt with a camera

5,001 Things for Kids to Do

1445. Keep an apothecary jar with personal treats on your desk
1446. Read about the Native Americans
1447. Read a textbook on geology
1448. Learn how to read palms
1449. String small beads into a delicate necklace
1450. Clean out under your bed
1451. Engage in barter
1452. Make clothespin people
1453. Make a combination pool shot
1454. List your loved and valued things
1455. Find out how big the universe is
1456. Write down a word with twelve letters and see how many smaller words you can make from it
1457. List all the things you can do with an empty tin can
1458. Collect shells for making necklaces
1459. Make a catnip toy for the cat
1460. Think up an idea for a new company
1461. Become a volunteer reading tutor
1462. Read about archaeology
1463. Discover new trails

1464. Study insect life

1465. Find out why we kiss under mistletoe

1466. Create your own wrapping paper

1467. Volunteer time at an animal shelter

1468. Bait your hook and catch a fish

1469. Store snowballs in the freezer

1470. Decorate your address book with doodles

1471. Update a fairy tale

1472. Make an album of special events

1473. Read about the United Kingdom

1474. Make a rain gauge

1475. Replace run-out batteries

1476. Do a cat's cradle

1477. Laugh at someone's jokes

1478. Become active in volunteer work

1479. Learn how to use a computer

1480. Open up the Bible randomly and read stories

1481. Weave a friendship bracelet

1482. Find out what happens to ink when newspapers
are recycled

1483. Make a hand puppet

5,001 Things for Kids to Do

1484. Read Ecclesiastes

1485. Jump rope

1486. Brush the dog's teeth

1487. Practice for an appearance on *Jeopardy!*

1488. Study photography

1489. Look at your baby pictures

1490. Make a list of books on your favorite subject that
you'd like to own

1491. Eat a silent meal

1492. Build a getaway tree house

1493. Make a folder for your drawings, doodles,
paintings, sketches, and photographs

1494. Save pennies and nickels; when the piggy gets full,
take it to the bank

1495. Make a mosaic

1496. Find your axilla

1497. Build a city of cardboard containers

1498. Read about glass and ceramics

1499. Wear edible jewelry

1500. Learn everything you can about the profession
you have chosen

1501. Do Slinky runs down the stairs
1502. Read about Noah's Ark and the
       Ark of the Covenant
1503. Make up your own core curriculum
1504. Read about he Babylonians
1505. Plant and raise a box garden
1506. Name Santa's eight reindeer
1507. Catch leaves floating down from fall trees
1508. Make a neighborhood Mardi Gras
1509. Sing the National Anthem at a sports event
1510. Read acknowledgments, introductions, and
       prefaces to books
1511. Hold a séance
1512. Ask God an important question
1513. Watch the goings-on in a busy harbor
1514. Chew gum and walk at the same time
1515. Experience being out in the rain
1516. Do something for others that also enriches you
1517. Practice Jim Carrey lines
1518. Choreograph a dance to a song
1519. Master the game of charades

5,001 Things for Kids to Do

1520. Make paper bag puppets
1521. Look for a feather on the beach
1522. Read a magazine
1523. Sew on your loose buttons
1524. Make posters for the bulletin board
1525. Make a collage cartoon
1526. Learn from a mistake
1527. Clean off your desk
1528. Feed the piggy bank
1529. Choose an Easter project
1530. Make a list of biodegradable items in the house
1531. Mow with the hand mower
1532. Hunt for buried treasure at the beach
1533. Build a snowman
1534. Do a falling front roll
1535. Study Native American art forms
1536. Read about the Pilgrims
1537. Read about navies
1538. Read about Julius Caesar
1539. Watch a real artist at work on a painting
1540. Create a treasure hunt with clever clues

1541. Wear a propeller beanie for a day
1542. Make a list of questions you'd like to ask someone
        you are just getting to know
1543. Invent something with as many uses as Velcro
1544. Watch a bird build its nest
1545. Make new friends
1546. Write a short story
1547. Adapt a novel for the movies
1548. Count the stitches on a baseball
1549. Listen to rhythm and blues
1550. Design a personal budget, and stick to it
1551. Make prints with fruits and vegetables
1552. E-mail the president of the United States
1553. Write a poem about winter
1554. Leap like a kangaroo
1555. Figure out why carpenter's pencils are square
1556. Ride a hobby horse
1557. Learn to identify the Earth's seas
1558. Collect pennies
1559. Read about telescopes
1560. Invent a bedtime story

1561. Paint a portrait

1562. Test a theory

1563. Make an obstacle course for your dog

1564. Read about the universe

1565. Make party favors and place cards

1566. Pick a one- or two-syllable word and think of all the words that rhyme with it

1567. Read a book

1568. Make a sci-fi mask of aluminum foil

1569. Explore a hidden world under a log

1570. Write to Bill Gates via bill@microsoft.com

1571. Study Buddhist or Hindu dharma

1572. Make coasters

1573. Create a picture you can eat from matzoh, honey, cereal, raisins, and nuts

1574. Read about the human body

1575. Find out about the origins of your house

1576. Write a letter using words cut out from a magazine

1577. Dry summer flowers for winter bouquets

1578. Practice dancing in front of a mirror

1579. Read about nuclear energy and the nuclear age

1580. Find out why nurses wear white
1581. Read up for a wilderness survival test
1582. Become an espionage agent
1583. Create beautiful fans for a hot summer day
1584. Get a bird's-eye view
1585. Memorize the numbers of all the players on your
       favorite MLB team
1586. Write a love letter to each member of your family
1587. Figure out if you're a morning person or night owl
1588. Stage an action figure battle
1589. Find out why cutting onions makes you cry
1590. Water the houseplants
1591. Set up a message center
1592. Build a kit that you got as a gift
1593. Learn to do needlepoint
1594. Wind up a jack-in-the-box
1595. Learn to identify the constellations
1596. Figure out what the clouds look like
1597. Be a back-up singer
1598. Change your hairstyle
1599. Know all the U.S. presidents—in order

5,001 Things for Kids to Do

1600. Read about migration
1601. Read about corals and how reefs are formed
1602. Slide down a sand dune
1603. Underline important points when studying notes for a test
1604. Organize a nature camp and charge admission
1605. Have a backward day
1606. Decorate your school notebooks
1607. Attend an event where you're a minority
1608. Plan a family reunion
1609. Do a trip journal
1610. Browse a picture book
1611. Keep a record of compliments you receive
1612. Explore a barn
1613. Corral dust bunnies
1614. Dust the top of the refrigerator
1615. Make bewitching facial expressions
1616. Make a stencil pattern
1617. Finish a reading list or assignment list
1618. Sit on the washer or dryer while it is going
1619. Have a picnic

1620. Organize your personal papers
1621. Put a message in a bottle and float it out to sea
1622. Make up some knock-knock jokes
1623. Try to predict what the Magic 8 Ball will say
1624. Find out when kids turn into goats
1625. Learn to make something beautiful with
       your hands
1626. Line up chairs to make a "train" or "airplane"
1627. Spin a paper plate on a stick
1628. Design costumes for a play or musical
1629. Create an artist's studio and prepare a one-person
       art show
1630. Recycle the junk mail
1631. Live without television
1632. Recycle paper
1633. Learn carpentry
1634. Set up an "office" for doing homework
1635. Put out a can to measure rainfall
1636. Become a Big Brother or Big Sister
1637. Make a tie rack
1638. Find your tragus

1639. Make coil pots out of hardening clay

1640. Do organic farming

1641. Make a collage of parts of pictures of yourself

1642. Learn tai chi

1643. Draw a Maserati

1644. Make a bird or animal feeder

1645. Read about the Vietnam War

1646. Bodysurf

1647. Donate canned goods for a food drive

1648. Find nests and burrows

1649. Sit with your eyes closed and try to identify small sounds

1650. Take a bubble bath in the middle of the day

1651. Do a maze

1652. Practice ballet

1653. Paint your wagon

1654. Weed out old books and magazines you don't need

1655. Raise a family of butterflies

1656. Read about horses

1657. Play with the big boys

1658. Make a chef's hat

1659. Learn to play castanets

1660. Take a bag of deposit bottles to the store
    to get the cash

1661. Learn the names of the different branches
    of medicine

1662. Make a folder for your journal, short stories, story
    ideas, trivia, and informal writing

1663. Invent a new candy bar

1664. Make a list of fads you have and
    have not followed

1665. Sort dirty clothes by color

1666. Practice for the National Spelling Bee

1667. Learn to tap dance

1668. Plan a project for your next snow day off school

1669. Write a thank-you letter to someone

1670. Solve Rubik's Cube

1671. Make a mobile with family pictures

1672. Time yourself in an activity and then keep trying to
    beat your time

1673. Listen to the sound of rippling and falling water

1674. Search for animal homes
1675. Count a cricket's chirps for fifteen seconds and add forty to get the temperature
1676. Hide and seek
1677. Watch parades on TV
1678. Donate a week's allowance to a charity
1679. Find out why humans are most comfortable at 72 degrees
1680. Eat fiber
1681. Make a recycling bin
1682. Make fingerprint cartoon characters
1683. Take apart an old, non-working telephone
1684. Figure out which is which: Jekyll and Hyde
1685. Write down all the foreign country capitals you can
1686. Give your pennies a bath in vinegar and salt
1687. Illustrate Mom's recipe cards
1688. Watch home movies or slides
1689. Make cards to hold up in a cheering section
1690. Write a note with your eyes closed
1691. Find out why zebras aren't ridden
1692. Make water balloons outside

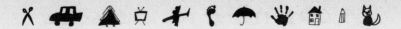

1693. Learn to box

1694. Work on brain teasers

1695. Read about gems and jewelry

1696. Cut paper dolls from shirt cardboard

1697. Write to the mayor to see if he/she will speak to your class

1698. Study stumps to learn the life history of a tree

1699. Pull someone around in a wheelbarrow

1700. Make a car for the soapbox derby

1701. Find out why women have higher voices than men

1702. Make Japanese lanterns out of construction paper

1703. Type up your favorite quote and put it where you can see it every day

1704. Write a how-to article

1705. Call the new kid in school

1706. Jazz up some sneakers with special shoelaces, glitter, buttons, markers, etc.

1707. Help someone overcome shyness

1708. Invent a new flavor of lollipop

1709. Find out why root beer has so much foam

5,001 Things for Kids to Do

1710. Watch the news
1711. Go bowling
1712. Count your freckles
1713. Capture the flag
1714. Learn ten bones of the body
1715. Tell fortunes with cards
1716. Pretend to host a weekly radio program
1717. Create a filing system for school papers
1718. Learn exactly how a car works
1719. Decorate a room for a party
1720. Find out why American electricity runs on AC
1721. Design an electronic house
1722. Find out why some cheeses are orange
1723. Start a dog-walking business
1724. Listen to the Brandenburg Concertos
1725. Browse through cookbooks
1726. Grab a handful of change and guess how much money you have
1727. Make a recipe for a magic potion
1728. Organize your baseball cards
1729. Learn how to send signals with a mirror

1730. Boil an egg

1731. Plan your next Halloween costume

1732. Watch a banana skin turn brown

1733. Learn the Heimlich maneuver

1734. Go on a mini archaeology dig in the backyard

1735. Pretend to be a ghost and play in ghostland

1736. Create architecture from Popsicle sticks

1737. Work an anagram

1738. Draw an object you see without lifting the pencil off the page

1739. Bake a coffee cake or muffin mix

1740. Put together a good basic traveling art kit

1741. Do percussion with spoon castanets

1742. Play the comb kazoo

1743. Explore what the world looks like from ground level

1744. Do an entire BrainQuest set

1745. Play a joke

1746. Learn affixes and their meanings

1747. Go to Speranza by reading *Robinson Crusoe*

1748. Learn the International Phonetic Alphabet

5,001 Things for Kids to Do

1749. Listen to Beethoven's nine symphonies
1750. Find out the name of the world's oldest
      living thing
1751. Find out how they get Teflon to stick to the pan
1752. Make book plates for your library
1753. Crack a secret code
1754. Imagine and draw the perfect giant space station
1755. Draw/color outside the lines
1756. Browse in antiques stores
1757. Find out why worms come out on the sidewalk
      after a rain
1758. Find out what keeps water in lakes and ponds
1759. Make bread in a bread machine
1760. Make up stories about the house where you never
      see anyone go in or out
1761. Sort things into your own classifications
1762. Make up an imaginary friend
1763. Spend a day in the countryside with a sketchbook
      and pen
1764. Construct a newspaper collage
1765. Learn what the number of train whistles mean

1766. Research a famous abolitionist

1767. Read about bridges and bridge building

1768. Feed the animals

1769. Write a poem about baseball using ten baseball terms

1770. Design a perfectly safe car

1771. Learn and use a new word each day

1772. See how long you can balance something on your head

1773. Find out why dogs don't get laryngitis from barking continuously

1774. Jog in place for ten minutes

1775. Tell your parents you love them

1776. Learn about each of the cultures in your community

1777. Teach your parents something you learned at school

1778. Find out how paper is made

1779. Find out why bun packages don't match hotdog packages

1780. Plan a going-back-to-school wardrobe

5,001 Things for Kids to Do

1781. Sing "99 Bottles of Beer on the Wall"

1782. Concoct clever combinations

1783. Draw with your eyes closed

1784. Join a book club

1785. Read about ancient Egypt

1786. Collect stamps

1787. Have lunch with your best friend from school

1788. Raise a bonsai

1789. Kick a habit

1790. Paint the pavement with water

1791. Do pull-ups

1792. Make believe

1793. Build a house out of toothpicks and peas

1794. Keep a list of all the books you've read

1795. Do Taps and Reveille on a kazoo

1796. Take your parents out for dinner

1797. Celebrate the birthday of a famous person

1798. Make paper bag "pets"

1799. Weed out the Halloween or Easter candy

1800. Read about oil

1801. Find out why there is no canned broccoli

1802. Race walk

1803. Find out why other people hear our voices
differently than we do

1804. Shoot wastebasket hoops

1805. Take a vacation with your pet

1806. Create a mural-sized family time line

1807. Find your way by the stars or by the sun

1808. Predict an event of the twenty-first century

1809. Compose a school song

1810. Sing every word of a grand opera

1811. Find out why poultry has white meat
and dark meat

1812. Find out why some keys go in right-side-up, some
upside-down, and why they aren't standardized

1813. Make no excuses for a day

1814. Clean out the refrigerator

1815. Start a journal or diary or list of things
to be happy about

1816. Do the "wave"

1817. Thank all your best teachers

1818. Play the harmonica

5,001 Things for Kids to Do

1819. Find out if fish sleep
1820. Find out why blue is associated with boys and
       pink with girls
1821. Try writing the alphabet backward and the letters
       in reverse
1822. Read about sound and sound recording
1823. Read all the cereal boxes
1824. Kick like a Rockette
1825. Tell someone's fortune
1826. Find out how three-way lightbulbs work
1827. Take your dog to a park or place where he/she
       can meet dog friends
1828. Search for a mirage
1829. Make mud pies
1830. Read the fine print on everything for one day
1831. Look up boborygmi
1832. Ask to read your parents' wedding announcement
1833. Snap your fingers
1834. Play in a bell choir
1835. Have a safari party
1836. List your ten favorite fast-food items

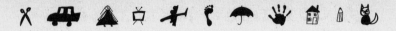

1837. Write a dramatic production and prepare to produce it

1838. Teach yourself to draw your favorite cartoon character

1839. Teach yourself to juggle with rolled-up socks

1840. Learn to e-mail a photo

1841. Take a compass bearing

1842. Sweep the porch, patio, walkway

1843. Listen to your parents

1844. Think up a great April Fool's joke

1845. Have a marble race

1846. "Adopt" a shelf at the library and make weekly visits to line up the books

1847. Dust the doll furniture and house

1848. Find out if there are programs or classes in the community where you can learn about money

1849. Frame a great report card

1850. Plan a carnival or puppet show

1851. Volunteer at the Special Olympics

1852. Plant a seed and watch it grow

1853. Distinguish between rocks and minerals

5,001 Things for Kids to Do

1854. Start a weekly newspaper about the family
   or the neighborhood

1855. Jot down the little things you want to accomplish

1856. Wait outside church when there's a wedding

1857. Read about air forces

1858. Put a bow on the cat or dog

1859. Read about the life of a lake

1860. Find a gear or pulley at work

1861. Memorize a list of the first ten objects you see
   when you wake up in the morning

1862. Build a dollhouse

1863. Prepare a frog for a frog-jumping contest

1864. Apply to be on a TV game show

1865. Make peanut brittle

1866. Find out why many farm plots are now circular
   instead of square

1867. Return everything you've borrowed

1868. Find out why Q and Z are missing from the
   telephone keypad

1869. Sort trash for recycling

1870. Climb a rope

1871. Master a miniature golf course

1872. Wrap a present beautifully

1873. Do sand casting

1874. Tell time using the twenty-four-hour clock

1875. Throw bread crumbs out for winter animals

1876. Go to the zoo

1877. Stroll among wildflowers

1878. Collect lost golf balls at a golf course

1879. Rename the planets and explain your "scheme"

1880. Find out how pretzels got their shape

1881. Write your will

1882. List your ten favorite buildings (and why)

1883. Compile facts and figures

1884. Make a string balloon

1885. Learn how to do a "proper" table setting

1886. Send the president a photo to autograph

1887. Build a puppet stage

1888. Get your room in apple-pie order

1889. Visit other places you have lived

1890. Costume a doll

1891. Sing around a pretend campfire

5,001 Things for Kids to Do

1892. Create personalized stationery

1893. Practice for the National Geography Bee

1894. Count birds for the local Audubon Society

1895. Put money in a mechanical bank

1896. Learn to change a tire

1897. Balance a book on your head for a half hour

1898. Straighten or curl your hair

1899. Find out why yawning is contagious

1900. Find out why insects are repelled by yellow light

1901. Write to Santa Claus via e-mail

1902. Walk on a rope

1903. Use your time creatively

1904. Make a list of things to sell at a garage sale

1905. Read about the Arabs and their history

1906. Practice going off the diving board

1907. Stitch an old-fashioned sampler

1908. Read about Islam

1909. Learn how to sharpen a penknife

1910. Organize a harmonica band or other
musical group

1911. Collect badges and pins

1912. Become a hula hoop champion

1913. Hug a tree

1914. Learn the aviation alphabet from alpha to zulu

1915. Pick a hobby you want to start and take
the first steps

1916. Walk a line back and forth and then do it sideways

1917. Do a single-color jigsaw puzzle

1918. Make a kite from a big paper bag

1919. Read your pile of magazines

1920. Find out why ants like sidewalks

1921. Pretend you are something you are not

1922. Draw your favorite dinosaur

1923. Study weather and make weather flags,
barometer, etc.

1924. Find out why newsprint yellows

1925. Make the planets to scale out of Play-Doh

1926. Learn pet first aid

1927. In the mirror, recite something you are
trying to learn

1928. Read about Germany

1929. Learn how to make fortune cookies

5,001 Things for Kids to Do

1930. Peel a grape

1931. Write down a recipe for excitement

1932. Let someone know you want to be their friend

1933. Know a thing or two

1934. Pretend you have a part on a soap opera

1935. Learn how to write the Greek alphabet

1936. Try to figure out what last night's dreams meant

1937. Look up tips for storing your comic books

1938. Go get the newspaper

1939. List the postal abbreviation of every state

1940. Practice your free throws

1941. Have a Closest to the Pin contest

1942. Read about the United Nations

1943. Make Silly Putty pictures

1944. Customize a doorknob hanger for your room

1945. Make clever luggage tags

1946. Skip a stone

1947. Learn fly-fishing tactics

1948. Master crossword puzzle-ese

1949. Find out why moths are attracted to light

1950. Do a cave painting

1951. Learn orienteering

1952. Make a flea trap

1953. Design something for the twenty-first century

1954. Learn to interpret character from handwriting

1955. Take your dad bowling

1956. Find out why angel food cake needs to be turned
upside-down while cooling

1957. Change something about the way you look

1958. Find the science that interests you most

1959. Jump up and click your heels together

1960. Invent words (sniglets) for things

1961. Learn the folklore regarding stars and
constellations

1962. Plant and raise a flower bed

1963. Write about a book you devoured

1964. Dance the Charleston

1965. Do a cryptic crossword

1966. Find out why hamburgers are so called when
there's no ham in them

1967. Take up astronomy

1968. Read about the Byzantine empire

5,001 Things for Kids to Do

1969. Invite someone to sleep over
1970. Design a chair or sofa
1971. Make up a word that everybody starts using
1972. Collect buttons
1973. Get something ready for show-and-tell
1974. Learn to recognize stars in the sky
1975. Look for shooting stars
1976. Pick a running mate for a student council run
1977. Nurse a sick animal back to health
1978. Make a nesting box
1979. Feed the pet(s)
1980. Read a joke book
1981. Create tissue paper roses
1982. Hang gadgets from a coat hanger for
        a unique mobile
1983. Write music while sitting at the piano
1984. Put together a travel toilet/beauty kit
1985. Do research on Lewis & Clark's journey and the
        sites where they stopped
1986. Do a pratfall
1987. Make a countryside or seaside collage

1988. Guess how much somebody/something weighs, then weigh them/it

1989. Assemble and fly a balsa plane

1990. Listen to a CB radio band

1991. Take a swim before supper

1992. Swim ten laps

1993. Start a standing ovation

1994. Make s'mores

1995. Take long walks with your pet (or jogs or hikes)

1996. Ask Jeeves a question on the Internet

1997. Make a hearty after-school snack

1998. Work on the school newspaper

1999. Find a berry

2000. Work on arts and crafts

2001. Shoot Nerf basketball

2002. Build with Tinker Toys

2003. Read an Ellery Queen mystery

2004. Find the letters you want in Alpha-Bits

2005. Give the dog off-leash time

2006. Go shopping

5,001 Things for Kids to Do

2007. Buy a souvenir

2008. Share a touching story

2009. Read when you are on vacation

2010. Eat an Oreo, filling first

2011. Visit an amusement arcade

2012. Get one jump ahead in school

2013. Boo when the Grinch steals Christmas

2014. Take a "yucky-day" hike

2015. Write an essay about good work ethics

2016. Put together a bag for beach going

2017. Call out the names on signs as you ride by

2018. Aid and abet a good deed

2019. Make a sandwich

2020. Beat your personal best

2021. Shop with someone

2022. Have a power breakfast

2023. Read *Good Night, Moon*

2024. Slip into a Jacuzzi or whirlpool

2025. Take your newspapers to an elderly neighbor each evening

2026. Leave voice mail

2027. Form a hypothesis
2028. Have a cookie and a cup of tea
2029. Give something away
2030. Walk the dog for a neighbor
2031. Buy someone a present
2032. Read *Disney Adventures* magazine
2033. Sit in a wading pool
2034. Make a TV dinner
2035. Let someone get ahead of you in line
2036. Eat at a diner
2037. Load new software
2038. Get ready for the big game
2039. Sunbathe
2040. Attend a party
2041. Eat all you want of a favorite food
2042. Go back to square one
2043. Admire someone's teeth
2044. Eat at an ice cream parlor
2045. Smell the rain
2046. Eat a tomato
2047. Nap on the beach

5,001 Things for Kids to Do

2048. Dive headfirst into a transparent pool

2049. Fall asleep in a beanbag chair

2050. Watch bubbles rise as water boils

2051. Watch a movie on video

2052. Cut your nails

2053. Go buy a double cheeseburger

2054. Take a nap in tall grass

2055. Roast marshmallows

2056. Send e-mail

2057. Keep your desk and work area neat

2058. Find the perfect gift for somebody

2059. Browse in stores

2060. Achieve a goal

2061. Make a bark rubbing with paper and crayons

2062. Go on a fun run

2063. Take a stroll through light rain

2064. Do power walking

2065. Go on a walking tour

2066. Find something weathered

2067. Think of activities you can do with friends other than "hang out"

2068. Open the lines of communication
2069. Dream of a better world
2070. Imagine the feel of swinging high on a swing
2071. Try something new
2072. Do things in the back of your mind
2073. Absorb information from books
2074. Save someone a place in line
2075. Learn to read tea leaves
2076. Put all your bookmarks in one place
2077. Clean up a campsite
2078. Do dancercize
2079. Read about the work of an anthropologist
       or archaeologist
2080. Use a clothing marker to label your camp and
       beach clothes
2081. Learn how to parallel-park your bicycle
2082. Do hand rhymes
2083. Pray
2084. Say grace
2085. Work on a new-interest project
2086. Feed your intellectual appetite

2087. Take a shower or bath
2088. Learn to spell
2089. Write down déjà vu experiences
2090. Offer to bring homework assignments to someone
      who is absent from school
2091. Explore back roads
2092. Start a "commonplace book"
2093. Collect comic books
2094. Count the petals of a daisy
2095. Articulate a problem and solve it
2096. Give up chewing gum
2097. Put healthy foods on the grocery list
2098. Read about veterinarians
2099. Listen to elevator music
2100. Practice pantomime
2101. Sample music of another decade
2102. Develop your own learning activities
2103. Finish unfinished business
2104. Imagine the feel of biting into an apple
2105. Pick a good cause to support
2106. Help someone with a guilt or inferiority complex

2107. Make a wish for the day

2108. Collect gum wrappers

2109. Soak up the latest gossip

2110. Read a book cover to cover in one sitting

2111. Touch-type

2112. Give a gift you made yourself

2113. Pick someone's brains

2114. March to a beat

2115. Put your watch on twenty-four-hour military time

2116. Collect buffalo nickels

2117. Think up something really clever for birthday
party favors

2118. Watch educational television

2119. Watch a situation comedy

2120. Spoil someone else

2121. Repair a broken friendship

2122. Reveal your deepest secret to your closest friend

2123. Tell someone you love that you really love them

2124. Give thanks before a meal

2125. Play with pull toys

2126. Read about theater

2127. Watch the sun rise

2128. Clear a writer's block

2129. Powder your nose

2130. Pretend you're playing the course at Pebble Beach

2131. Meet a deadline

2132. Repeat the Pledge of Allegiance

2133. Sing at bedtime

2134. Learn to improvise

2135. Dub a tape

2136. Cover a shoe box with an assortment of stickers

2137. Learn to pronounce Himalayas

2138. Change your operative word

2139. Take poetic license

2140. Forgive someone you are mad at

2141. Instill hope in someone

2142. Do something to maintain or improve your health

2143. Surprise someone with a smile

2144. Find something yourself; don't give up

2145. Be someone's cheerleader

2146. Take up the hobby of writing

2147. Do breathing exercises

2148. Wiggle your toes

2149. Eat a healthy breakfast

2150. Jot things down in notebooks that are always around

2151. List twelve Christmas stocking stuffers

2152. Ask outrageous questions

2153. Listen to the birds singing outside

2154. Talk to your pet(s)

2155. Have an original thought

2156. Refresh someone's memory

2157. Learn in the summertime

2158. Shoot the breeze

2159. Do creative thinking—all day

2160. Learn English in fun ways

2161. Scratch a pet behind the ears or under the chin

2162. Inspire someone

2163. Imagine the smell of toothpaste

2164. Write on water

2165. Dress down

2166. Blow a kiss to someone

2167. Learn to play pool

2168. Study with a friend; give each other quizzes

2169. Set your alarm clock

2170. Leave a note for someone in a funny place

2171. Imagine the taste of peanuts

2172. Imagine the sound of a car starting

2173. Play with pull-back cars

2174. Rehearse for a test

2175. Take a breather

2176. Imagine the smell of gasoline

2177. Clear a mental block

2178. Put your nose in a book

2179. Listen to the wind and the birds

2180. Break the ice

2181. Get involved

2182. Envision how you want something to go at school or a special event

2183. Pretend you're riding the Orient Express

2184. Wish upon a star

2185. Raise the blinds in the morning

2186. Roar back at the ocean

2187. Read about tanks

2188. Read about building
2189. Take apart an old Etch-a-Sketch to see
how it works
2190. Meet friends at the ice cream stand
2191. Buy a treat at the grocery store that won't spoil
your dinner
2192. Remember what you read
2193. Plan an interesting walk
2194. Write down serendipitous occurrences
2195. Play soft music
2196. Read about the Stone Age
2197. Walk the dog
2198. Sing Christmas carols
2199. Help someone with a homework problem
2200. Share a book you enjoyed
2201. Read a book that makes you think
2202. Lower the blinds at nighttime
2203. Read about the history of farming
2204. Help someone practice
2205. Read extra books
2206. Browse through books in the house

5,001 Things for Kids to Do

2207. Do yoga

2208. Learn to have fun on your own

2209. Enjoy a dew-drenched morning

2210. Talk to a family member

2211. Hear birds sing praises for a new day

2212. Start the ball rolling on something

2213. Ask the Magic 8 Ball some questions

2214. Buckle down to work

2215. List all the different kinds of Barbie dolls you know

2216. Observe bees pollinating flowers

2217. Play

2218. Explore the wonders and miracles of nature

2219. Practice a sport you're good at

2220. Smell the pages of a new book

2221. Put something extra in someone's piggy bank

2222. Clap to a beat

2223. Give someone a second chance

2224. Plan to climb a mountain

2225. Clap for Tinkerbell

2226. Learn a new game of Solitaire

2227. Read more books

2228. Hug a pillow
2229. Write down five rules you think everyone
should obey
2230. Exercise vigorously
2231. Study maps
2232. Try to guess the meaning of a word from the way
it is used
2233. Enjoy the full extent of nature, books, pictures, music
2234. Dazzle someone
2235. Nap on a lazy Saturday
2236. Give a new friend your phone number
2237. Imitate a voice from a Walt Disney cartoon
2238. Make a wall hanging out of felt
2239. Memorize a rebus dictionary
2240. Write a pilot for a soap opera
2241. Serenade someone
2242. Begin each day with your favorite music
2243. Roll up the rug and dance
2244. Tap out a message in Morse code
2245. Make a banner to hang up at a professional
sports event

2246. Get a paper route

2247. Write in a stream of consciousness

2248. Learn to make candles

2249. Record your dreams

2250. Concentrate on listening to all the sounds around you

2251. Help prune, feed, and repot houseplants

2252. Start a diary you'll really enjoy keeping

2253. Do an art project using three different media or techniques

2254. Wear primary colors

2255. Learn the true meaning of the holidays

2256. Read about George Washington

2257. Start a watermelon garden

2258. Make different shapes with five toothpicks

2259. Look at bark with a magnifying glass

2260. Take a younger child to story hour

2261. Shave a peach

2262. Hide under your bed

2263. Take up gardening

2264. Water the plants

2265. Organize the doll clothes
2266. Kick or hit or bounce a rubber ball
2267. Guess how long the driveway is, then measure it
2268. Make a list of things you did on vacation
2269. Have a counter lunch
2270. Call your favorite radio DJ
2271. Find out why X stands for kiss
2272. Make a clothesline
2273. Read a primer on fly fishing
2274. Read a Nancy Drew mystery
2275. Read about the potter's art
2276. Design a purse or wallet
2277. Write someone's biography for the school paper
2278. Teach a cat to brush its teeth
2279. Film a day in the life of your family
2280. Find out why pirates wore earrings
2281. Memorize the international road signs
2282. Have a free-throw shooting contest
2283. Clean up for someone else
2284. Read about the phenomenon of heat
2285. Make refrigerator magnets

5,001 Things for Kids to Do

2286. Raise your ecological consciousness
2287. Put out nesting material for birds
2288. Mentally rearrange the furniture in your room
2289. Complete a really tough maze
2290. Go on a pretend lion hunt
2291. Read about the alphabets and learn one totally
      different from the Roman alphabet
2292. Write a slogan
2293. Memorize your favorite poem
2294. Rename all the fifty states
2295. Try to beat the Guinness world record
      for skipping stones
2296. Make amends to those you've harmed
2297. Read about the land and people of the Caribbean
2298. Read your Bible
2299. Pretend you are ruler of the world
2300. Ride through a park
2301. Wear suspenders
2302. Read about X rays
2303. Try not to blink for five minutes
2304. Make moving puppets with brads

2305. Be a pet detective
2306. Use plastic containers and tin cans to build a
rocket ship
2307. Find out how a book is made
2308. Write a message in code
2309. Whistle
2310. Memorize birthdays and anniversaries
2311. Read about bicycles and motorcycles
2312. Make plaster casts of tracks in mud
or at the beach
2313. Learn a cool "magic number" trick
2314. Send for a free gift or brochure
2315. Take up butterfly collecting
2316. Reflect
2317. Visualize a favorite place
2318. Read about the Eskimos
2319. Learn how to read a map
2320. Learn how to hand-squeeze orange juice
2321. Sew an outfit or clothing item
2322. Send your best recipe to the local newspaper
2323. Have a tea party

2324. Pretend you're emceeing the Grammys

2325. Learn to Rollerblade

2326. Go kitchen camping under a table with a
blanket over it

2327. Emcee the evening's entertainment

2328. Sing camp songs

2329. Learn origami

2330. Learn to do the samba

2331. Identify your mission in life

2332. Wear a secret decoder ring

2333. Adopt a tree and get to know it

2334. Build a miniature golf course

2335. Learn to dribble a basketball like a pro

2336. Learn how to tie a bow tie

2337. Study the insides of things

2338. Rename your street

2339. Look for opportunities to make people
feel important

2340. Learn ventriloquism

2341. Have a game party

2342. Read about Scandinavia and its history

2343. Make a paper necklace from a postcard
2344. Do carpet bowling
2345. Make pipe cleaner people
2346. Tie a stack of newspapers the right way
2347. Scream for your team
2348. Earn an Eagle Scout badge
2349. Recite three tongue twisters
2350. Cut out paper snowflakes
2351. Make up a limerick
2352. Smell all the different spices in the spice cabinet
2353. Teach yourself to be ambidextrous
2354. Run or jog for ten minutes
2355. Make a mask from a cereal box
2356. Make a list of books everyone should read
2357. Offer to walk a dog
2358. Read about mammals
2359. Organize an exercise class
2360. Read about gravity
2361. Get your hands dirty
2362. Invent your own transportation vehicle and
          name it

5,001 Things for Kids to Do

2363. Read a book in a bubble bath
2364. Learn the origin of your town's name
2365. Read biographies of successful men and women
2366. Write a sonnet
2367. Learn to recognize poison ivy, poison sumac, and poison oak
2368. Find your own philosophy
2369. Read a book about birds
2370. Draw or paint pictures of wildflowers
2371. Build a radio set
2372. Lead a sing-along
2373. Buy a special decoration for your room
2374. Find out why paper cuts hurt more than other cuts
2375. Use a piece of rope for a lasso
2376. Have an English breakfast
2377. Involve yourself in a local political campaign
2378. Wash your sneakers and dry them in the sun
2379. Go to a children's museum
2380. Learn reflexology
2381. Race two Slinkys down the steps
2382. Make a map of the town

2383. Pretend you're umpiring a major league game
2384. Name as many pouch-type (marsupial) animals
as you can
2385. Communicate with animals
2386. Sharpen your pencils
2387. Using a basketball or playground ball, do a bounce
pass, a chest pass, and a baseball pass
2388. Do a front roll
2389. Read about Christopher Columbus
2390. Learn to waltz
2391. Make a "guess the number of" jar
2392. Learn a song and dance
2393. Try making five triangles using only
nine toothpicks
2394. Take a virtual tour of a castle
2395. Ask for what you want
2396. Plan your dream vacation
2397. Pick up shells for a collection
2398. Snoop around the basement
2399. Read about zoos and how they're run
2400. Read a chemistry textbook

5,001 Things for Kids to Do

2401. Make a dispenser for a ball of string
2402. Design a desk
2403. Do a virtual tour of archaeological sites
2404. Count your Beanie Babies
2405. Try to make a video of yourself displaying a talent
2406. Make up a story using pictures in a magazine
2407. Learn to speak French
2408. Dress like what you want to be when you grow up
2409. Take an aromatherapy bath
2410. Learn the metric system
2411. Create comic strips starring your family
and friends
2412. Read about ports and waterways
2413. Make a wish and throw a penny in a fountain
2414. Have a mystery party
2415. Study computer science
2416. Train for the triathlon
2417. Learn to tie an overhand knot and a square knot
2418. Read about Italy
2419. Watch a movie or TV show about a
historical event

2420. Find out why some ladybugs don't have spots

2421. Come up with a balancing act

2422. Conduct a trash brigade, cleaning up the yard
or neighborhood

2423. Label your toys with a Sharpie marker

2424. Back up your hard drive

2425. Invent a game that becomes popular

2426. Hang the clothes out on a clothesline

2427. Make a life-size replica of yourself

2428. Make a list of *Encyclopaedia Britannica* articles you
want to read

2429. Find out why the tiniest safety pins are gold

2430. Dissect a raspberry

2431. Learn how to operate a laptop computer

2432. Create personalized brown paper lunch bags

2433. Find out why bike tires go flat if you don't use
them for a while

2434. Sneak up on an animal

2435. Hit Wiffle ball homers

2436. Make sure all the clocks and watches are set on
the exact same time

2437. Squirt a squirt gun for distance

2438. Read tarot cards

2439. Hide goody bags and write riddles for the guests
    to find them

2440. Drink a coconut

2441. Build an elaborate structure from Popsicle sticks

2442. Think about something you really believe is true—
    and try to prove that you're wrong

2443. Assemble a newspaper hat

2444. With another person, make up a story, taking turns

2445. Rig a pole with line and attach a hook, bobber,
    and sinker

2446. E-mail the celebrity you admire most

2447. Enter something in the state fair

2448. Learn to recognize different fish species

2449. Read about architecture

2450. Make your own fashion magazine

2451. Find out why the sun looks yellow

2452. Learn some Chinese and Japanese

2453. Cheer for a team

2454. Look for faces in the clouds

2455. Browse through library books

2456. Polish your charm bracelet

2457. Sign up for a fishing derby

2458. Repair an old clock

2459. Put Velcro strips on something

2460. Design gift baskets

2461. Read about pirates

2462. Pick flowers, with permission

2463. Snowshoe

2464. Call a friend

2465. Find out why so many Irish names start with *O'*

2466. Read about castles of yore

2467. Set up a Lionel train

2468. Watch the sunset

2469. Make a sand painting

2470. Play a sport

2471. Do a running commentary

2472. Salute the flag

2473. Make relief maps

2474. Give your pet time and affection

2475. Chase a rainbow

5,001 Things for Kids to Do

2476. Put your own "stamp" on the way you do things

2477. Learn to send secret messages

2478. Tighten all the screws in the house

2479. Leave flowers on the doorstep of a neighbor

2480. Plan an aquarium: what you'll need and the money

2481. Learn to recognize different kinds of soil

2482. Write a story about summering in a villa in Tuscany

2483. Create your own birdseed mix

2484. Rent movies of your favorite actor or actress

2485. Make a paper bag piñata

2486. Collect things during a walk

2487. Decorate a picture frame with ribbon

2488. Learn collective nouns

2489. Read about China

2490. Try to figure people out

2491. Clean the inside of Mom or Dad's car

2492. Recognize the phases of the moon

2493. Throw a surprise birthday party for a friend

2494. Dance alone with the lights out

2495. Learn to write by reading a lot
2496. Help a disabled child
2497. Window-shop on the Internet
2498. Create reverse silhouette art
2499. Find out why police lights flash red and blue
2500. Find out what *cottage* means in
    cottage cheese
2501. Learn acoustic guitar
2502. Make your own lunch
2503. Make a plant box
2504. Weave a twine or plastic lanyard key chain
2505. Go roller skating
2506. Doodle
2507. Make breakfast in bed for someone
2508. Forage for food in the wilderness
2509. Watch an engine at work
2510. Invent a floor surface that never needs cleaning
2511. Rent a video game
2512. Develop your own barbecue sauce recipe
2513. Make a college out of Hershey's Kisses
2514. Hide nice little surprises

2515. Read a magazine like *Nickelodeon* or *GeoWorld*
or *Dig* or *Sports Illustrated for Kids*

2516. Try to keep a goldfish alive a year

2517. Pretend to be a spin doctor

2518. Be a beach bum for an afternoon

2519. Make a snowman and hope it doesn't melt
for a week

2520. Scribble a creative expression of your feelings

2521. Enjoy the magic of an old-fashioned toy
like a Whee-Lo

2522. Learn to dog paddle

2523. Eat asparagus

2524. Play (carefully) on the porch steps

2525. Read about and make a cylinder seal

2526. Write notes with a metallic-ink or invisible-ink pen

2527. Read the *Boy Scout Handbook* or
Girl Scout Handbook

2528. Pick out a new backpack for back-to-school

2529. Imagine going on a blind date

2530. Talk your parents into throwing out all the play guns

2531. Read late at night, with permission

2532. Watch a funny infomercial
2533. Watch Saturday morning cartoons
2534. Finish a project before it is due
2535. Plan ahead and break a school project into manageable "bites"
2536. Put a photograph of each person of your family in a collage
2537. Have a "longest-drive" contest with plastic golf clubs and balls
2538. Look up a number in the phone book rather than call directory assistance
2539. Write up a blow-by-blow account of your day
2540. Throw rotten fruit out into the woods
2541. Do two hundred sit-ups
2542. Learn cool ice cube tricks
2543. Write down uplifting quotations
2544. Put on a minstrel show
2545. Set up a guessing game
2546. Discover all the family secrets
2547. Make a flint tool
2548. Learn to yodel

5,001 Things for Kids to Do

2549. Have a Beanie Baby tea party

2550. Eat cereal without sugar

2551. Perform the five positions of classical ballet

2552. Kick a beach ball

2553. Cut out paper dolls

2554. Hold a quilting bee

2555. Read an exciting adventure story

2556. Write and illustrate a book

2557. Play with a typewriter

2558. Have an indoor parade

2559. Draw a picture from a favorite fairy tale

2560. Be a sidewalk artist

2561. Create your own couplets

2562. Find out why there are eighteen holes on a golf course

2563. Make a bird-feeding bell

2564. Make letter trays

2565. Write a play for children

2566. Learn the longest word in English

2567. Value learning for its own sake

2568. Blow bubbles and keep them from popping
       or landing

2569. Set your radio alarm so you can get up on time

2570. Collect kindling for the fireplace

2571. Change the containers you keep toys in

2572. Spend time with a brother or sister

2573. Create the bathroom of your dreams

2574. Try to envisage what the world will be like when you're grown up

2575. Beat a path to someone's door

2576. Learn what the squiggles on top of chocolate candies mean

2577. Find out why graves are six feet deep

2578. Find out if woodpeckers get headaches

2579. Play with your brother's or sister's toys

2580. Construct a war game

2581. Make a slingshot

2582. Visit a stable

2583. Add a fashion patch to an item of clothing

2584. Set up balloon races

2585. Do an energy survey of your home and reduce consumption by 10 percent

2586. Go watch a nearby sporting match

2587. Imitate bird calls

2588. Read about the climates

2589. Mold gelatin

2590. Watch water quietly lapping

2591. Watch a Fred Astaire-Ginger Rogers movie

2592. Read about the history of transportation

2593. Decorate your Frisbee

2594. Read about South America

2595. Eat Girl Scout cookies

2596. Study the martial arts

2597. Find out why glue doesn't get stuck in the bottle

2598. Make a necklace

2599. Become an ace Frisbee player

2600. Learn how to fly an airplane

2601. Take "slice of life" pictures

2602. Wash all the windows

2603. Read historical fiction

2604. Experience the thrill of going barefoot

2605. Read about submarines

2606. Make a list of fifteen things you like to do and choose to do when you get the chance

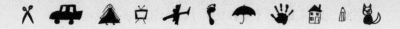

2607. Make a TV-watching schedule for the week

2608. Find out why ham doesn't change color
   when cooked

2609. Throw cards into a hat and keep trying to beat
   your score

2610. Plan an outpost camp

2611. Write your thoughts on doing away with child,
   drug, substance, and sexual abuse

2612. Draw pictures to describe events

2613. Run up and down a football field or soccer field

2614. Look at all your View-Master reels

2615. Find a pure white rock

2616. Collect Pez dispensers

2617. Plan and lay out an adventure trail

2618. Find inspiration in a work of art

2619. Design toys

2620. Name the seven dwarfs

2621. Find out why Oreos are called Oreos

2622. Make breakfast for someone

2623. Do crayon rubbings

2624. Read about earthquakes

2625. Tutor someone in your best subject

2626. Read the thirteen sequels to *The Wizard of Oz*

2627. Create an item of clothing from paper

2628. Walk with a book on your head for five minutes

2629. Organize your room

2630. Make a wall plaque

2631. Practice ballet steps

2632. Help organize an Earth Day celebration

2633. Paint your toenails and/or fingernails

2634. Turn cleaning the house into a game

2635. Put your music collection in alphabetic order

2636. Eat prunes

2637. Find the origin of *odds and ends*

2638. Go get the mail

2639. Read about the wind

2640. See a pure sky at dawn and sunset

2641. Visit a news dealer

2642. Learn to draw

2643. Play dolls

2644. Make a hygrometer

2645. Read a Scrabble dictionary

2646. Learn how to use your watch as a compass

2647. Learn cool vanishing coin tricks

2648. Devise paper airplanes and decorate them

2649. Get familiar with the telephone directory

2650. Use new paints

2651. Read about tunnels

2652. Paint diagrams of the heavens on dark paper with luminous paint

2653. Clean your room

2654. Find out what makes popcorn pop

2655. Ghost-write for someone

2656. Collect old and funky keys

2657. Make a magnet/paper clip fishing game

2658. List foods in each of the four basic food groups

2659. Document your life with photos

2660. Read about the wonders of the ancient world

2661. Go for a walk

2662. Find out your state flower, bird, insect, tree, and motto

2663. Mix honey and mayonnaise for a fruit-dipping sauce

2664. Study "combining forms"

2665. Memorize a poem by Walt Whitman

2666. Read about the ancient Persians

2667. Create personal letterhead on the computer

2668. Devise a way to organize the pots and pans

2669. Take a day trip to an aquarium

2670. Learn cool disappearing tricks

2671. Practice for an athletic event

2672. Make a pinwheel

2673. Keep a special notebook with beautiful things in it

2674. Know your planet and learn how it works

2675. Do research on the Internet

2676. Read the *Adventures of Huckleberry Finn*

2677. Buy your fish a new plastic plant

2678. Invent a new language

2679. Do your chores without being reminded

2680. Pick a new color scheme for the computer

2681. Write a letter to the president

2682. Be an interior designer and build in 3-D on paper

2683. Draw a picture of yourself doing the kind of job
        you'd like when you grow up

2684. Dictate your stories or write them into a notebook
2685. Listen to opera on the radio
2686. Find a picture, glue to stiff paper, and cut into a puzzle
2687. Stage a dude ranch rodeo
2688. Study hieroglyphics
2689. Start a conversation
2690. Hold a garage sale
2691. Drink eight glasses of water a day
2692. Keep a record of the lessons you learn
2693. Go to the circus
2694. Take a trip to collect materials for nature crafts
2695. Read about light and all its uses
2696. Start a project or plan an event for your youth group
2697. Choose your life's work
2698. Find out how they keep the raisins from falling to the bottom of cereal boxes
2699. Take a parent to lunch
2700. Call someone on the telephone
2701. Learn what the animal world has to teach

2702. Rent a tandem bicycle with a friend

2703. Determine the one thing in life you want most

2704. Look things up like "turbo" that you've always wondered about

2705. Plan an exotic feast using a cookbook you find at the library

2706. Prepare to enter the Soapbox Derby

2707. Write down the trees you see in a day

2708. Pretend you're riding on the Concorde

2709. Recycle a bicycle

2710. Be in two places at once

2711. Take a woodworking class

2712. Explain definite and indefinite article

2713. Build the *Titanic* out of toothpicks

2714. Garden

2715. Start a snow-shoveling or leaf-raking business

2716. Do something in a different room than you usually do it in

2717. Learn Esperanto

2718. Self-publish a book

2719. Set up a movie theater and show a video

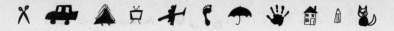

2720. Find your childhood blanket, doll, or comforter

2721. Grow something in a petri dish

2722. Ride a horse

2723. Make an Advent calendar

2724. Write a letter or story

2725. Write a set of directions for a parent to follow

2726. Have a sprinkler party

2727. Find out why all calico cats are female

2728. Figure out what New Age is

2729. Decorate a gift box

2730. Make the longest list of opposites you can

2731. Read a funny book or magazine

2732. Have a watermelon seed spitting contest

2733. Think of three ways to make where you live more beautiful

2734. Try to hypnotize the cat

2735. Listen to the four Mozart horn concertos

2736. Count cars of different categories on the road

2737. Become an entrepreneur

2738. Plant flowers

5,001 Things for Kids to Do

2739. Make different faces, substituting hairstyle
      and features
2740. Drink dandelion tea
2741. Wish on a star
2742. Make your own trail mix
2743. Learn cool dollar bill tricks
2744. Find out why the underside of a baseball cap visor
      is usually green
2745. Tumble
2746. List all the things that bug you
2747. Teach the dog to wipe its feet
2748. Keep a list of your job ideas
2749. Memorize the preamble to the U.S. Constitution
2750. Make up limericks using place names on signs
2751. Pretend you're a Hollywood agent
2752. Walk on your hands
2753. Impress your friends by knowing odd superstitions
2754. Enter a beauty contest
2755. Make a vase
2756. Contribute to the Salvation Army
2757. Become a kids' organization expert

2758. Build a tabletop terrarium
2759. Run for office in an organization
2760. Study the biographies of the people you
   most admire
2761. Campaign to save the manatees
2762. Find out why some eggs are white
   and others brown
2763. Write a letter to an older person
2764. Read the labels of all the food boxes and cans
2765. Be a Scout leader
2766. Do your own desktop publishing
2767. Cover your books with paper protectors
2768. Plunk a banjo
2769. Have a meeting of the minds
2770. Find out why rain doesn't come down
   a chimney
2771. Watch a Western movie
2772. Find out why fly swatters have holes
2773. Weave a wreath of flowers
2774. Have a football toss and pretend you're
   a famous quarterback

5,001 Things for Kids to Do

2775. Make a list of non-biodegradable items in the house

2776. Work on the school, team, or Scout fund-raiser

2777. Write a restaurant review of the last place you ate—or of your mom's cooking

2778. Take a long walk

2779. Talk mushy to your boy/girlfriend

2780. Figure out what Worcestershire sauce is

2781. Travel back through time

2782. Find out why Good Friday is so named

2783. Make a list of twenty things that would be in "the perfect place"

2784. Load the dishwasher

2785. Show off a new feat

2786. Make a ring

2787. Plan a bell-ringing ceremony

2788. Learn cool egg tricks

2789. Memorize the numbers of the players on your favorite NBA team

2790. Make a paper doll chain

2791. Turn over a rock and observe the fauna living underneath it

2792. Gallivant around

2793. Let your pet have private time

2794. Work on becoming a world-famous
      fashion designer

2795. Give your pet a mini-spa treatment

2796. Learn to download a photo

2797. Create neat anagrams

2798. Try brussels sprouts

2799. Read old *National Geographic* magazines

2800. Go through the alphabet, writing down five
      adjectives for each letter

2801. Explain the difference between an equinox
      and a solstice

2802. Collect animal figures

2803. Look out a window and draw the scene—as a
      different season

2804. Learn to bake bread

2805. Find out why there are no purple Christmas lights

2806. Attend someone else's religious or
      cultural celebration

2807. Watch the world go by from a sidewalk café

5,001 Things for Kids to Do

2808. Learn to write your name in Chinese characters
2809. Sew a fancy appliqué on socks
2810. Find something that floats
2811. Smile at a baby
2812. Wrap a package so it is neat and tight
2813. Keep in touch with relatives far away
2814. Find out why elections are held on Tuesdays
2815. Make decorations for a holiday
2816. Find out why flush handles are on a toilet's left
2817. Become a great punster
2818. Send a "thinking of you" card
2819. Go fly a kite
2820. Find out why there aren't seat belts in buses
2821. Use a gift certificate
2822. Study geology
2823. Read about the Crusades
2824. Read about democracy
2825. Interview your grandparents about their lives
2826. Volunteer at a shelter
2827. Sponsor a needy child
2828. Meet your pen pal

2829. Study earth sciences
2830. Find out why starving children have bloated stomachs
2831. Find tracks
2832. March in a parade
2833. Dress up
2834. Learn five new places on a map
2835. Practice legible handwriting
2836. Draw a picture of yourself winning out over your greatest fear
2837. Clean out the birdcage
2838. Capture a great moment on camera
2839. Keep a daily log of the wonders you experience
2840. Make a waffle and decorate it with cherries, banana, etc.
2841. Take up interval training
2842. Read a rule book
2843. Be a personal trainer for your mom
2844. Write to a friend in invisible ink
2845. Camp on a doorstep
2846. Make a banjo

5,001 Things for Kids to Do

2847. Get off your high horse

2848. Cooperate

2849. Figure out the name of the restaurant you will open someday

2850. Float around a lake in a raft

2851. Dip everything in Cool Whip for one meal

2852. Go up and down the stairs twenty times

2853. Find a frog for a jumping contest

2854. Guess animal life spans, then look them up

2855. Join a book group

2856. Cheer for your sister or brother

2857. Make a periscope

2858. Name the eight wonders of the world

2859. Study drum rhythms

2860. Cut out a silhouette of someone

2861. Learn enough Italian to order in a restaurant

2862. Go an entire day without eating any sugar

2863. Design a greeting card for Hallmark

2864. Learn to write fancy like John Hancock

2865. Find out why twenty-one was chosen as the age of adulthood

2866. Sign up as a volunteer
2867. Conduct a local Academy Awards ceremony
2868. Give a toy to a child less fortunate
2869. Come up with a family motto
2870. Go through catalogs and make your birthday or Christmas list
2871. Attend an opening night
2872. Complete a craft project
2873. Use empty soda bottles to make a bowling game
2874. Use the word *pediatrician* and see how many words of at least three letters you can make
2875. Get in touch with a former life
2876. Wiggle your ears
2877. Join a singing group
2878. Make herbal tea
2879. Take time exposures of stars with a camera
2880. Clean all the baseboards in the house
2881. Build a green cathedral/outdoor chapel
2882. Hug an old Cabbage Patch doll
2883. Make a list of things in piles
2884. Reread your favorite book

5,001 Things for Kids to Do

2885. Practice your putt
2886. Do hopscotch
2887. Pretend you're a TV commentator
2888. Figure out what a mixed metaphor is
2889. Rub two sticks together and start a fire
2890. Prepare for a concert or recital
2891. Commit yourself to constant self-improvement
2892. Practice fancy block capitals
2893. Find out why pepper makes us sneeze
2894. Sort out your junk bin or drawer
2895. Find out why a mile is 5,280 feet
2896. Make a whisk broom
2897. Prepare a pretty bread basket
2898. Look like a million dollars
2899. Invent an outdoor game
2900. Pamper your pet
2901. Feed birds in the winter
2902. Figure out a better way to do something
2903. Organize a bike parade
2904. Construct a water slide
2905. Coach a friend in your best sport

2,906. Ride a Big Wheel or scooter

2,907. Decorate paper plates for the next family meal

2,908. Learn how to influence the content of your dreams

2,909. Read the fine print on everything

2,910. Learn all the bones of the body

2,911. Break a bad habit

2,912. For a half hour, use no words, only signs
and gestures

2,913. Suck the filling out of a Twinkie

2,914. Cut up six-pack rings to help save fish
and seabirds

2,915. Make your own fishing pole, bait, and lines

2,916. Find out how the first day of a season
is determined

2,917. Talk to the shyest person in school

2,918. Have a spoon race

2,919. Get involved in an environmental organization

2,920. Come up with silly substitutes

2,921. Make someone's acquaintance

2,922. Visit someone else's school or church

2,923. Do string painting

5,001 Things for Kids to Do

2924. Find out why we eat ham at Easter

2925. List six foods you would never eat

2926. Lay out your clothes for tomorrow

2927. Write to the celebrity you most admire

2928. Learn a hog call

2929. Feed the worms

2930. Display your Happy Meal/Kid Meal toys

2931. Name eight tools in the house and what they do

2932. Find out why lobsters turn red when boiled

2933. Memorize phone numbers

2934. Make a landscape painting of your town

2935. Create an engraving

2936. Pretend that your bicycle is a car

2937. Run in slow motion

2938. Lower your voice

2939. Make a Mobius strip

2940. Design your own . . .

2941. Figure out how to do something all by yourself

2942. Learn to recognize five kinds of bird eggs

2943. Get an older person to tell you a story

2944. Become a crime writer

2945. Study the rules of euchre

2946. Submit a Boy Scout or Girl Scout application

2947. Figure out why it is called an Adam's apple

2948. Make an experiment work

2949. Read about Antarctica and the Arctic

2950. Go to Middle-earth via *The Hobbit* or
Lord of the Rings

2951. Read about balloons and airships

2952. Straighten something that is crooked

2953. Warm your socks

2954. Read about how the ears work

2955. Teach yourself to be ambidextrous

2956. Wear team colors on game days

2957. Toss a pair of dice and record the results
of each roll

2958. Go dancing

2959. Knead bread

2960. Attend a town meeting

2961. Count the holes in a Saltine cracker

2962. Stare at a corner of a room for thirty seconds,
write down everything you saw, and check it

2,963. Create a diorama with a peephole in one end

2,964. Pitch a tent and camp in it

2,965. Be queen or king for a day

2,966. Learn an interesting African dance and teach it to your friends

2,967. Work on a snow sculpture

2,968. Make a camping trip master list

2,969. Leapfrog

2,970. Send a fan letter anonymously

2,971. Make a tape of your favorite songs

2,972. Review a movie

2,973. Make alien pictures

2,974. Think of connections between seemingly unrelated items

2,975. Climb a fence, without ripping your pants

2,976. Think about how history would be different if an important event had not happened or was changed

2,977. Look up what "week" it is (Cleaner Air Week) and do something in commemoration

2,978. List favorite candies in order

2979. Develop your own artistic impulse

2980. Create a graph for checking off your chores

2981. Walk a treadmill

2982. Do shuffleboard

2983. Put on a vaudeville show

2984. Choreograph a ballet

2985. Create a trivia game with questions about your family members and special family events

2986. Find out why golf balls have dimples

2987. Help with yard work

2988. Find out why so many perfumes are yellow

2989. Understand photosynthesis

2990. Pick an object and list all the things you could possibly do with it

2991. Mix food coloring or paints to make different colors

2992. Pick a painting and turn it into a story

2993. Plan a surprise party

2994. Wear two different earrings

2995. Make a gingerbread house

2996. Read the Brontë sisters books

5,001 Things for Kids to Do

2,997. Sharpen all your pencils

2,998. Make up your own spaghetti sauce

2,999. Work on problem-solving and
decision-making skills

3000. Join a soccer team

3001. Program the VCR

3002. Talk in your best Irish brogue

3003. Read the mail addressed to "occupant"

3004. Breed a hybrid flower

3005. Collect all the Beatles' recordings

3006. Hug yourself

3007. Memorize stats for the starters on your
favorite team

3008. Clean your pet's teeth and ears

3009. Go on a secret hiding place hunt

3010. Create a bed or nook for your pet

3011. Research the chamber of commerce, tourism
office, or travel information bureau for your
next destination

3012. Complete a jigsaw puzzle

3013. Sing a song to the pace of the windshield wipers

X 🚙 🏕 📺 🤾 👣 ☂ 🖐 🏠 ✏️ 🐈

3014. Have an egg toss

3015. Learn the Latin alphabet

3016. Knit a Christmas stocking

3017. Sketch with pastel crayons

3018. Gather different-colored stones

3019. Collect cattails and marsh grasses for nature crafts

3020. Look for weeds in the garden

3021. Read about polar exploration

3022. Study your ethnic background

3023. Write a letter to get Ken to have realistic hair

3024. Think about how many windows there are in your house . . . doors . . . chairs . . . closets

3025. Draw a picture of the night sky, mapping the stars you see

3026. Find out why people don't get goose bumps on their faces

3027. In a wish bank, save money for something you want

3028. Write a plan of action for a business you want to start

3029. Bob for apples

3030. Use Briticisms in your speaking
3031. Watch a cloud being "born"
3032. Remember someone's birthday
3033. Make up a holiday you want your family
      to celebrate
3034. Sled
3035. Use a pulley
3036. Get a literary agent for your writing
3037. Study the travels and discoveries of Darwin
3038. Learn to play croquet
3039. Make up a new Jelly Belly flavor
3040. Throw out bread crumbs for the birds
3041. Put together a craft box
3042. Pretend you are a tightrope walker on a rope on
      the floor
3043. Read *The Old Farmer's Almanac*
3044. Watch boats on a lake
3045. Read about the Netherlands
3046. Get into the swing of things
3047. Start a writers' colony
3048. Have a picnic lunch on a blanket

3049. Chart your moods in relation to the moon phases
3050. Use a mnemonic to remember things you have to do
3051. Draw a person without them knowing it
3052. Eat a whole box of broccoli in one sitting
3053. List the things you could do to improve where you live
3054. Think of what you would do if you had only three months to live
3055. Make a secret compartment in your desk
3056. Do a half hour of stretching exercises
3057. Find the recipe for the best chocolate cake in the world
3058. Write a rap song
3059. Train for a marathon
3060. Become a book reviewer
3061. Make a yarn-covered vase
3062. List ten reasons why you are important to your family
3063. Read one encyclopedia article per day
3064. Sing your brother or sister to sleep

3065. Draw little pictures for amusement
3066. Pretend you are playing the stock market and plan your investments
3067. Write a letter
3068. Read about aircraft
3069. Collect money for a charity
3070. Make paper flowers
3071. Watch shows that improve your vocabulary or math skills
3072. Convert inches to centimeters
3073. Deliver newspapers on Rollerblades
3074. Find out the origin of penny loafers
3075. Make a coin-rubbing picture
3076. Find out about Mensa and take practice tests
3077. Do nature photography
3078. Find out if George Washington ever spent time in your neighborhood
3079. Pick a stage name
3080. Create a good filing system
3081. Practice skateboarding
3082. Decorate the top of a box with shells

3083. Surprise loved ones with little gifts
3084. Practice the shot that will win the game
at the buzzer
3085. Prepare a costume box for your next play
3086. Have a sock hop in the den
3087. Plan a space station
3088. Learn computer assembly language
3089. Find out why leather is so expensive
3090. Take a hike
3091. Create a space odyssey
3092. Feed the birds
3093. Practice intricate hand shadows
3094. Give overused words a break and substitute
synonyms for them
3095. Sell the most items for a fund-raiser
3096. Create a vacation information library
3097. Try a face-painting kit
3098. Remember everything you read
3099. Work on scrapbooks and stamp or
snapshot albums
3100. Start a collection count for your treasures

5,001 Things for Kids to Do

3101. Find a way to make money to help buy the things you want
3102. Build an outdoor theater
3103. Dress up an army of GI Joes
3104. Learn to speak some sentences in another language
3105. Try to draw something that's on a magazine cover
3106. Practice for an egg-and-spoon race
3107. Learn to use chopsticks
3108. Punch a punching bag
3109. Create a homemade musical instrument
3110. Be a pen pal
3111. Build a sand city
3112. Teach a recipe to a friend
3113. Slide
3114. Arrange a tea and book club for Saturday mornings
3115. Become a Civil War buff
3116. Study something till you know it, then surprise everyone
3117. Set up a hundred cowboys and Indians

3118. Build a six-foot snowman
3119. Write a comedy
3120. Make a display of miniatures
3121. Create a secret code
3122. Play GI Joe
3123. Turn on some music and sing along
3124. Read about scientists and inventors
3125. Replace a button
3126. Pick a favorite hymn
3127. Dance in front of a mirror
3128. Read a book on manners
3129. Pretend you're summering in the Swiss Alps
3130. Bake gingerbread
3131. Do roller printing (a pattern over and over)
3132. Teach the family a new game
3133. Eat sugar-free for a day
3134. Cut sandwiches into different geometric shapes
3135. Make up a clever acronym
3136. Learn cartography
3137. Win at Scrabble without cheating
3138. Experiment with mixing colors

3139. Make a list of invertebrates you have seen
3140. Memorize the periodic table
3141. Have a talent show
3142. Figure out when you last used the rights in the
       First Amendment
3143. Fax your best friend
3144. Take up reflexology
3145. Master the jungle gym
3146. Be a slave for a day, doing chores for someone else
3147. Find out why ancient cities are buried in layers
3148. If you don't know how to spell a word, look it up
       in a dictionary
3149. Find out why peanuts grow in pairs in the shell
3150. Learn one great card trick
3151. Mark a path and make a trail
3152. Pick interesting music for musical chairs
3153. Experiment with fashion styles
3154. Pick a sport and create a safety checklist
3155. Find the best place in hide-and-seek
3156. Make a recycle collage from leftover/thrown-out
       grocery products

3157. Plan and lay out an obstacle race

3158. Start a family sing-along

3159. Clean your hairbrush

3160. Find out what makes the holes in Swiss cheese

3161. Have a tug-of-war with the dog

3162. Make a glove puppet

3163. Ride your bike

3164. Read about the first books

3165. Take the Mensa test

3166. Find out how they print M&M on M&M candies

3167. Look for secret recipes on the Internet

3168. Create a Zen garden

3169. Somersault

3170. See if you know anyone who likes fruitcake

3171. Fish a stream

3172. Make a pop-up card

3173. Sign up for a correspondence course/home study

3174. Make a marionette

3175. Start a letter you can add to each day

3176. Put a collection of treasures on your desk

3177. Compose a perfect haiku

3178. Give the pet a grooming or beauty treatment

3179. Organize a littler pickup or litter patrol

3180. Predict the next movie blockbuster

3181. List the superstitions you believe in

3182. Practice kung fu

3183. Learn to knit

3184. Do a "man in the street" interview with someone you know

3185. Review a music CD

3186. Do a cartwheel

3187. Find out why the sky is blue

3188. Listen to shortwave radio

3189. Read about making iron and steel

3190. Subscribe to a magazine for cat or dog lovers

3191. Climb trees

3192. Make your own stencils

3193. Bury "treasure" for the dog in an area where it is allowed to dig

3194. Act out a play with someone

3195. Use new words you learn right away, especially in a sentence in normal conversation

3196. Go to a complete newsstand and buy a foreign magazine

3197. Learn the difference between a count and uncount noun

3198. Hit tennis balls against a backboard

3199. Read about Abraham Lincoln

3200. Gain an understanding of how a particle accelerator works

3201. Watch a cat stalking a bird

3202. Make a hiking stick

3203. Read about the aboriginal Australians

3204. Dance to music on the radio

3205. Conduct your own "geological survey"

3206. Measure the time it takes for an ice cube to melt

3207. Read about the continent of Asia

3208. Pretend you're at the Indianapolis 500

3209. Master ventriloquism

3210. Have an amateur night

3211. Go an entire day without getting angry

3212. Cut and paste

3213. Design packaging

3214. Learn about low-impact, no-trace camping

3215. Go outside and do something physical

3216. Go on a virtual tour of the White House

3217. Write an acceptance speech for an award you want to earn

3218. Record your thoughts or feelings in a journal or diary

3219. Engage in small talk

3220. Find out how ducks stay warm in cold water

3221. Coin a phrase

3222. Help paint a room

3223. Roll like a rolling pin down a hill

3224. Draw a butterfly from a specimen

3225. Earn a badge in scouting

3226. Challenge a computer to a game

3227. Make a list of itinerary ideas for your next vacation

3228. Imagine you are an astronaut when you go high on a swing

3229. Name the capital of as many states as you can

3230. Feed your stuffed animals with play food

3231. Send an anonymous valentine

3232. Compose a hit song
3233. Make up a name for a club you want to form
3234. Try to piece together what an ancient ruin used to look like
3235. Knit a winter cap
3236. Try to get on a radio discussion show
3237. Prepare a list of important telephone numbers for yourself
3238. Pretend you're a super hero or romantic heroine
3239. Learn to play "Amazing Grace" on the piano
3240. Go rock climbing
3241. Do library research
3242. Weed the garden
3243. Frame a picture
3244. Make a leaf stencil
3245. Construct a model
3246. Think up a name for a newspaper column you want to write
3247. Do happy dancing
3248. Make a harvest basket
3249. Challenge yourself with a new software program

3250. Practice hitting ground balls

3251. Brainstorm

3252. Make a yarn doll

3253. Try to find work related to a specific talent or interest you have

3254. Listen to the Beethoven piano sonatas

3255. Make cool labels for your file folders

3256. Read about astronauts

3257. Roll up the garden hose neatly

3258. Learn macramé

3259. Learn to tango

3260. Name five cars that are no longer made

3261. Listen to an air-traffic-control radio band

3262. Read about military engineering

3263. Collect nuts, pinecones, shells, seeds, milkweed pods, and twigs for a collage

3264. Play "elevator" in a closet

3265. Fool around on the piano

3266. Read about helicopters

3267. Write to a historical commission about a landmark's preservation

3268. Define your American dream
3269. Build characters or structures from canned beans
and toothpicks
3270. List all the berries you can think of
3271. Create a rag bag from old clothes
3272. Read about the Reformation
3273. "See into" a picture
3274. Find a knight in shining armor
3275. Get news from the Internet
3276. Find out how lasers work
3277. Make a bread sculpture
3278. Carve your initials on a tree
3279. Arrange family photos for a special occasion
3280. Buy a new paint box
3281. Write an essay about touring a famous home
3282. Select a category and try to think of things that fit
into it
3283. Make an exercise area for an indoor pet
3284. Follow Columbus's and Leif Eriksson's trips
to America
3285. Learn to twirl, dip, and delay a Frisbee

3286. Clean out your backpack

3287. Ride a scooter

3288. Design a family activity calendar with stickers

3289. Work toward joining Mensa

3290. Create an Etch-a-Sketch masterpiece

3291. Have a family picnic supper on the living room floor

3292. Send a funny story or original joke to a kids' magazine

3293. Learn how planes stay up

3294. Tie your shoelaces with a square bow knot

3295. Ask why bus windshield wipers work different than a car's

3296. Practice to beat a Guinness world record

3297. Practice celebrity impressions

3298. Dust off an old game and give it another try

3299. Make macaroni jewelry

3300. Make a nice CD holder

3301. Build a volcano in a plastic bottle

3302. Read about telephones

3303. Read about wilderness survival

3304. Find out why towels have a smoother and a more textured side

3305. Have a picnic with your stuffed animals
3306. Invent a way to generate inexpensive, non-polluting energy on a large scale
3307. Draw your shadow on the sidewalk
3308. Read about Alexander the Great
3309. Draw a picture of your fantasy airplane
3310. Read about the Ottoman empire
3311. Wash the car windows
3312. Write in runes
3313. Make a traveling crayon rubbing kit
3314. Write a story about when you lived in another time period
3315. Find out why dogs have wet noses
3316. Volunteer at the mayor's office
3317. Do a back roll
3318. Read about the art of papermaking
3319. Experiment with new ideas
3320. Draw cartoon faces
3321. Send away for a free pet care booklet or other publication
3322. Jump hurdles

3323. Decorate the mailbox for the next holiday

3324. Pin the tail on the donkey

3325. Name a star for someone as a birthday gift

3326. Make your Gak last longer

3327. File your school papers

3328. Make an accordion book

3329. Learn about circuit breakers

3330. Make sun tea

3331. Canoe

3332. Compose a new cheerleading yell

3333. Record a book on tape for someone blind or disabled

3334. Read a magazine you never looked at before

3335. Collect all the unused clothes hangers

3336. Be able to consistently hit four of five at the free-throw line

3337. Make a clothespin from twigs

3338. Do baby-sitting/get a baby-sitting job

3339. Read up on foreign affairs

3340. Find out how calories of food are measured

3341. Read a fairy tale

3342. Organize a voter registration drive
3343. Decorate mini pizzas with "faces"
3344. Design a custom car
3345. Do step aerobics
3346. Transform autumn leaves into winter mulch
3347. Make a crown of flowers
3348. Find a nice box or other container to display a
       collection in a neat way
3349. Fill out a time line with the major events
       of your life
3350. Switch roles for ½–1 day with another person
3351. Dance to zydeco
3352. Read about hibernation
3353. Make animals from pipe cleaners
3354. Dig in a sandbox
3355. Draw faces on your fingers for a finger
       puppet show
3356. Read an *Uncle John's Bathroom Reader*
3357. Make a list of topics you'd like to research
3358. Learn embroidery
3359. Produce your own talk/interview show

3360. Keep lookout from a tree

3361. Gain some exposure to great works of music

3362. Offer to work for free at a job related to your chosen profession

3363. Make a daisy chain

3364. Set up relay races

3365. Try to sell something

3366. Do a domino knockdown

3367. Collect items to sell at a church bazaar

3368. Invent something to patent

3369. Create a visual dictionary "entry"

3370. Try to make bubbles in things other than water

3371. Work on a stand-up comedy routine

3372. Pretend you are an explorer

3373. Grow an aloe plant

3374. Play slot cars

3375. Start a secret diary

3376. Do a crossword puzzle as fast as you can

3377. Clean your glasses

3378. Read old *Boys Life* magazines

3379. Polish your shoes

3380. Grow seeds in jars

3381. Open a new box of sixty-four Crayolas

3382. Paint the walls of your mind with beautiful pictures

3383. Help a parent organize the garage

3384. Follow a set of footprints

3385. Touch every third fence post down the street

3386. Pretend you've been invited to dinner at
       Buckingham Palace

3387. Figure out where your nares are

3388. Write a screenplay to send to Steven Spielberg

3389. Redesign the human body for greater efficiency

3390. Tease a cat playfully

3391. Have a naval battle in the bathtub

3392. Make a willow whistle

3393. Learn how to say hello in three other languages

3394. Find spelling mistakes in a newspaper

3395. Learn to play soccer

3396. Plan a carnival

3397. Find out why Whoppers have the numbers 1–12
       on the wrappers

3398. Learn to read a river

3399. Read parts of the *Oxford English Dictionary*
3400. Put together a hiking kit so you're ready to hike any time
3401. Rearrange your room
3402. Take a painting or drawing course
3403. Read about the Pacific Islands
3404. Pick out your favorite constellation
3405. Prepare custom car designs
3406. Do a workout tape
3407. Make crowns for the next family birthday
3408. Do all your chores
3409. Make a project or display for a fair
3410. Have a friend over
3411. Meet someone after school and do something special
3412. Send flag signals
3413. Try to write your name on a piece of paper placed on your forehead
3414. Come up with new words to a tune
3415. Make a train out of connected shoe boxes
3416. Make a trinket box

3417. Scratch someone's back so they will scratch yours
3418. Polish your Hot Wheels and Matchbox cars
3419. Do calisthenics
3420. Touch and smell trees
3421. Sink a three-pointer
3422. Make regular paper look like you found it
in an old chest
3423. Try to make a dream a reality
3424. Make finger puppets and prepare a show
by the cast
3425. Bird-watch out the window
3426. Read the last paragraph of every book
in the house
3427. Hunt for a four-leaf clover
3428. Get paint color samples from the hardware store
3429. Find out why our palms and soles don't
get sunburned
3430. Shake the rugs outside
3431. Stage a battle with plastic army men
3432. Identify nut-bearing bushes and trees
3433. Test your skills in track and field

3434. Create storyboards for a commercial

3435. Dare to play Truth or Dare

3436. Learn backgammon

3437. Color the sidewalk with chalk

3438. Study Aristotle's philosophy

3439. Throw horseshoes

3440. Read Trivial Pursuit cards

3441. Read about shells

3442. Mountain bike in a local park

3443. Go to the library and check out a book

3444. Put your books in alphabetical order or
      arrange by subject

3445. Have a dance party

3446. Explain the difference between skim and
      nonfat milk

3447. Design a briefcase

3448. Dress up with grandparents' old clothes

3449. Put all new stuff on your bulletin board

3450. Lick the beaters

3451. Celebrate the holiday of some other nation

3452. Put on a slide presentation

3453. Read about the Assyrians and their empire

3454. Have an evening campfire and star study

3455. Find horse chestnuts at the park

3456. Study a life science

3457. Teach a younger brother or sister
       something important

3458. Learn to play a harmonica

3459. Read Ellery Queen mysteries

3460. Prepare for a wilderness survival test

3461. Study mathematics

3462. Read about capitalism and communism

3463. Read about military aircraft

3464. Get an anti-monster flashlight

3465. Trim the hedges

3466. Pick the lint off your clothes

3467. Run your own business

3468. Paint pottery

3469. Test the soil pH

3470. Work on a disappearing magic trick

3471. Read about monasteries

3472. Clear a path

3473. Learn about contemporary health issues, such as AIDS

3474. Read a type of book you never did before, like science fiction

3475. Take close-up or zoom photos of animals (stalk with a camera)

3476. Do a printmaking project

3477. Grow a prize-winning vegetable

3478. Compose magnetic poetry on the refrigerator

3479. Find little words hidden in big words

3480. Pretend you're a great defense lawyer arguing a case

3481. Help plan, prepare, and cook an outdoor meal

3482. Learn all the bicycle safety rules

3483. Mix two cereals together for a meal

3484. Paint the sets for a play

3485. Put together a program of games, singing, and skits

3486. Make a sandbox where your dog will be allowed to dig

3487. Stage a fashion show

3488. Pretend you live in an Italian Riviera villa
3489. Put signs and buttons and comics on
    your bulletin board
3490. Collect menus
3491. Spritz the plants with water
3492. Make a rock bridge across a creek
3493. Read signs backward
3494. Make a pile of things you never use that can be
    given away or sold
3495. Learn to draw in perspective
3496. Cut out cardboard shadow puppets and put them
    on sticks
3497. Jog ten blocks
3498. Make static electricity and shock someone
3499. Go bird watching
3500. Learn the ropes
3501. Do flower arrangements
3502. Plant a herbaceous border
3503. Make homemade soda from fruit juice and
    sparkling water or club soda
3504. Repot a plant

5,001 Things for Kids to Do

3505. Visit houses on the National Register of Historic Places

3506. Do op art and pop art

3507. Read about armies

3508. Learn a Groucho Marx impression

3509. Read about World War I

3510. Read about navigation

3511. Lower your cholesterol

3512. Read five magazines at the library

3513. Grow magic rocks

3514. Practice trick basketball shots

3515. Read about the Minoans

3516. Design your dream house

3517. Make your own calling cards

3518. Draw in a sketchbook

3519. Make a hex sign to ward off bad spirits or bring good luck

3520. Find out the size of your "personal space"

3521. Attend a poetry reading

3522. Create a kewpie doll

3523. Study a foreign language

3524. Start your own Internet business

3525. Build a go-cart

3526. Try out for the cheerleading or pep squad

3527. Find out why clocks run clockwise

3528. Read all the magazines in the house

3529. Carve a jack-o'-lantern

3530. Teach yourself a calligraphy hand

3531. Find a walking stick, clean it, and decorate it

3532. Make an anemometer

3533. Teach yourself to play guitar

3534. Sit in the car and pretend to drive

3535. Throw a barn dance

3536. Give a rose to someone

3537. Make the ultimate peanut butter sandwich

3538. Write down things you think children should be
punished for and why

3539. Go ice skating

3540. Find a seed pod

3541. Teach a parrot to talk

3542. Organize restaurant donations of leftovers
for the homeless

3543. Invent a salad dressing

3544. Make a miniature machine

3545. Ride a stationary bicycle

3546. Send e-mail to a friend

3547. Make a Christmas tree ornament

3548. Listen to a classical album and make believe you are the orchestra conductor

3549. Have a monologue

3550. Find something to smile about

3551. Cut pictures you like out of magazines

3552. Learn the Arabic alphabet

3553. Make a list of ideas for inventors

3554. Find out what animals have eyes in the back of their heads

3555. Write down your beliefs

3556. Work on a science fair project

3557. Learn cheerleading yells

3558. Write and illustrate an alphabet book for a younger, less privileged child

3559. Write a children's book

3560. Take people's pictures with a Polaroid and sell them

3561. Organize your crayons by color

3562. Look for birds' nests

3563. Use a squirt gun on all the outdoor plants

3564. Do ten pages of homework

3565. Put together a sensible wardrobe

3566. Make a list of things you're grateful for

3567. Read *Drawing with Children* by Mona Brookes

3568. Exercise for fun

3569. Invent a replacement for dental floss

3570. Experiment with food coloring

3571. Learn to tie a necktie

3572. Find your name on the Internet

3573. Find out why the air is still just before
       a tornado strikes

3574. Read about airports and visit one

3575. Set five goals for the year

3576. Build a fort

3577. Look at the world upside-down

3578. Apply decoupage to a planter

3579. Take a plant you grew at school and transplant it
       in the garden

5,001 Things for Kids to Do

3580. Make a table decoration

3581. Find out why hyenas laugh

3582. Bake a banana

3583. Figure out your family's average life expectancy

3584. Run a six-minute mile

3585. Spin a top

3586. Make a "Swiss Army notebook" with paper, games, reading, and more

3587. Make a set of your own fingerprints

3588. Do your own greeting card for the next birthday or holiday

3589. Grow corn in the backyard

3590. Search for a rare plant species

3591. Subscribe to a special-interest magazine for kids

3592. Practice trick shots at the pool table

3593. Draw a famous caricature

3594. Have an arm wrestling contest

3595. Put on a puppet show

3596. Do a household Gallup poll

3597. Study lichens, mosses, and ferns

3598. Study a phrase book for a foreign country you want to visit

3599. Write about things you really know about

3600. Write a play

3601. Start a painting or collage fest on the kitchen table

3602. Decorate white T-shirts

3603. Create a nature collage

3604. Plan a boy-girl party

3605. Study technical drawing

3606. Figure out where your talents lie

3607. Listen to your favorite tapes or CDs

3608. Hang up your clothes

3609. Make a list of all the symbols you see in a day— written, worn, in art, and identification

3610. Build a sand castle or dirt city

3611. Gather fall leaves and preserve them

3612. Bike down dirt roads

3613. Collect acorns from the lawn so they don't get mowed

3614. Read about myths and legends

3615. Pitch a tennis ball against a backboard or safe large wall

3616. Practice learning to type

3617. Sort the nails in the tool box according to size

3618. Paint a mural

3619. Master your tennis serve

3620. Juggle scarves

3621. Help fix a meal

3622. Skip stones

3623. Write a short history of your community

3624. Read about Aristotle's philosophy

3625. Make an edible "house" of graham crackers, chocolate bars, marshmallows, and peanut butter

3626. Learn to use the *Reader's Guide to Periodical Literature*

3627. Make a bracelet of safety pins

3628. Clean out the litter box

3629. Count the Band-Aids

3630. Paint portraits

3631. Create a graffiti board for your room

3632. Decide what you want to be when you grow up

3633. Set short-term and long-term goals

3634. Ask the Ouija board some questions

3635. Take up abstract sculpture

3636. Make a Nerf football spin

3637. Make a collage of your baby pictures

3638. Design the perfect bed

3639. Watch a bud open

3640. Build a miniature replica Stonehenge

3641. Write down the plants you see in a day

3642. Put the kitchen spices in alphabetical order

3643. Complete all the tasks on your to-do list

3644. Make a glossary for your hardest
       school subject

3645. Make a rattle for a baby

3646. Keep a weather log

3647. Raise a caterpillar to become a butterfly

3648. Make a list of the things you accomplished in the
       last year

3649. Learn to tell time "military style"

3650. Separate die-cast cars by make, model,
       color, or type

3651. Learn to groom an animal

5,001 Things for Kids to Do

3652. Practice camp-craft skills
3653. Read the introduction to the dictionary you use
3654. Watch bees pollinate flowers
3655. Create a secret handshake
3656. Learn archery
3657. Read a nonfiction book
3658. Go berry picking
3659. Make Kachina dolls
3660. Design a skyscraper
3661. Serve as an altar person
3662. Learn how to juggle
3663. Take an advanced class
3664. Write an opinion about affirmative action
3665. Write a fairy tale
3666. Beat Dad or Mom at something
3667. Create a sundae bar
3668. Memorize the moons of every planet
3669. Pick a password for your fort or hideout
3670. Write a science fiction novel
3671. Keep up a "Row Your boat" round for five minutes
3672. Learn to sew

3673. Write out your seven favorite meals in menu form
3674. Draw an entire town
3675. Look for traces of animals
3676. Put together a period costume
3677. Wear a mask all day
3678. Find something symmetrical
3679. Bake homemade cat treats
3680. Design a lamp
3681. Read about the sun
3682. Do acrobatics
3683. Help get a bad law changed
3684. Make an art stash: markers, paper, crayons, scissors, tape, etc.
3685. Learn to type fast
3686. Go to a slot-car track
3687. Draw all the different kinds of windows you can think of
3688. Pan for gold
3689. Create a new sign language
3690. Start a reading group
3691. Write a potential best-seller

5,001 Things for Kids to Do

3692. Stage a Beatles marathon
3693. Investigate the attic
3694. Read a trivia book
3695. Learn to shuffle cards like a professional
3696. Campaign for someone
3697. Read about the Vikings
3698. Make a visual family tree
3699. Help preserve a landmark
3700. Write to the relative who lives farthest away
3701. Find out why doughnuts have holes
3702. Make a desk tray from clay
3703. Clean your ears
3704. Surf the Internet
3705. Read about Mexico
3706. Stage a reenactment
3707. Study the rules of etiquette
3708. Try selling your riddles to a magazine
3709. Learn to imitate an unusual animal noise
3710. Run a model railroad
3711. Write up the past week in your diary
3712. Plan tin can bowling

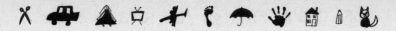

3713. Make a list of what you think are the top twenty inventions of all time

3714. Remember all the words to "The Twelve Days of Christmas"

3715. Hold a dance marathon

3716. Use an atlas program to create customized maps of places you'll be visiting

3717. Skate

3718. Find out why potato chips are curved

3719. Look at the details of a leaf in bright sunlight

3720. Wear your clothes backward for a day

3721. Polish your trophies

3722. Cast the movie of your book

3723. Learn how to use a rod and reel

3724. Dress a Barbie doll

3725. Read Greek myths

3726. Visit a dried-up streambed

3727. Clean the aquarium

3728. Design a menu for a make-believe restaurant

3729. Design a playground

3730. Design a board game

3731. Play with mechanical toys
3732. Read about glaciers and ice caps
3733. Read about the continent of Africa and its
       fifty-two nations
3734. Color Easter eggs
3735. Study art
3736. Learn the difference between a hopping print and
       a wading print
3737. Find out the difference between French and
       Italian bread
3738. Locate true north
3739. Count sheep
3740. Brush or groom the cat or dog
3741. Watch a caterpillar hatch into a butterfly
3742. Write a speech or oral book report on
       index cards
3743. Decide what to do if you win the lottery
3744. Get to know the reference librarian
3745. Find out why a twenty-one-gun salute has
       twenty-one guns
3746. Plan a hypothetical trip to the core of the Earth

3747. Figure out how far you can see from your house
3748. Role-play with friends
3749. Write a letter to your three favorite TV, movie, or sports stars
3750. Learn baseball score-keeping abbreviations
3751. List ten construction toys
3752. Meditate
3753. Decorate the cake(s) for a birthday party
3754. Make a scratching post for the cat
3755. Learn tricks with a Jacob's ladder
3756. Randomly put dots on a page and connect them to make a picture
3757. Find out why warm milk makes you sleepy
3758. Send a valentine
3759. Learn how to lasso
3760. Walk like different animals
3761. Do tin can craft
3762. Catch leaves as they fall from the trees
3763. Write down thoughts, ideas, inspirations, and practical tips
3764. Put on a shadow play

3765. Find numbers of things in a room that correspond to numbers 1 through . . .

3766. Be a role model for a younger person

3767. Draw your idea of the abominable snowman

3768. Emulate a great artist or scientist

3769. Make a map from one hundred years ago (facsimile)

3770. Create something with a hammer, nails, and scraps of wood

3771. Read about women's rights

3772. Play explorer

3773. Make a "socktopus"

3774. Create a toy for the cat

3775. Read C. S. Lewis's *Chronicles of Narnia*

3776. Draw a complicated cross-section

3777. Make your own crosswords, starting with a big word

3778. Study the auroras australis and borealis

3779. Pretend you're vacationing on a Pacific island

3780. Tiptoe all day

3781. Practice making sound effects

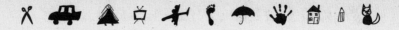

3782. Play with space toys
3783. Find out why it is warmer in the city than in the suburbs/outlying areas
3784. Paint a glass plate as an art project
3785. Create your own cartoon character
3786. Be a cowboy/cowgirl for a day
3787. Take time to look at the intricacy of spider webs
3788. Write a book report
3789. Be a princess/prince for a day
3790. Try to catch a minnow in a cup
3791. Recline on a futon
3792. Sort your clothes by type and color
3793. Learn to use the card catalog in the library
3794. Find out the difference between a rock, stone, ore, and mineral
3795. Find an early childhood toy
3796. See fog blown inland from the sea
3797. Read about the Revolutionary War
3798. Read about New Zealand
3799. Chalk a poem on the sidewalk
3800. Read something by Shakespeare

5,001 Things for Kids to Do

3801. Plant tomatoes and radishes
3802. Learn five mnemonics
3803. Create travel stickers representing places
    you've been
3804. Swing on a tire swing
3805. Read about an interesting subject,
    like computer programming
3806. Kazoo
3807. Make a wish list of toys
3808. Find a site on the Internet to view a tourist spot
3809. Learn the Morse code
3810. Plan a small business you would like to start
3811. Make snow cones
3812. Search for a genuine arrowhead
3813. Write down all the roles you play (who are you?)
3814. Watch an ant colony at work
3815. Find three different kinds of grass
3816. Make earrings
3817. Clean your Rollerblades
3818. Find out why the dessert baked Alaska
    was so named

3819. Make bark boats
3820. Find out the difference between a bun and a roll
3821. Learn all the verses of a hymn
3822. Take apart a Lego village
3823. Read the comics
3824. Make a peanut butter-bird seed bird feeder
3825. Design on paper something you want
        to build outside
3826. Pick a pen name
3827. Compile a life list of birds observed
3828. Write a story about being a stowaway
3829. Practice your Frisbee moves
3830. Sing in a choir
3831. Prick a balloon
3832. Read about atoms and molecules
3833. Decorate a juice can for a flower pot
3834. Dress up in a costume
3835. Dry summer flowers
3836. Find out how a rainbow is formed
3837. Read about the Wild West
3838. Fill and bury a family time capsule

3839. Write down some words, then see how many new words you can make by rearranging the letters

3840. List all the foods you know are yellow

3841. Create ceramics

3842. Use a thesaurus

3843. Learn bowling terms and scoring

3844. Work on attaining the next level or first level in a martial art

3845. Create a "me" poster with pictures from magazines of things you like

3846. Find out why roosters crow in the morning

3847. Roller-skate in the basement

3848. Make a rubber band guitar

3849. Write down all your important questions

3850. Hide under a bed and see if anyone misses you

3851. Find out the difference between a commonwealth and a state

3852. Learn to speed-read

3853. Lay out an orienteering course

3854. Make a sock puppet family

3855. Paint a stone paperweight

3856. Make a bookmark

3857. Make a bracelet

3858. Mark the dictionary every time you
      look up something

3859. Ride a rocking horse

3860. Separate necklaces, rings, and earrings in the
      jewelry box

3861. Weave garlands

3862. Draw gadgets

3863. Start a Chia Pet

3864. Build a kite from a kit

3865. Toot a tune on a bottle

3866. Make a potpourri for a natural air freshener

3867. Find out why dogs eat standing up and cats eat
      sitting down

3868. Write a story about an imaginary dive
      to the ocean floor

3869. Build up your biceps

3870. Color an entire coloring book

3871. Read about the Aztecs

3872. Read about Easter Island

3873. Draw Ionic, Doric, and Corinthian order temples
3874. Find out why bagels have holes
3875. Peek under the hood of the car and name
     the parts
3876. Shag softballs
3877. Make labels for things in your room
3878. Dress up like a storybook character
3879. Think up a nickname for yourself, your siblings,
     or your best friend
3880. Make a miniature zoo
3881. Design jewelry
3882. List all the games you know two people can play
3883. Make an electromagnet
3884. Pick a century and study all aspects of it
3885. Shoot a bow and arrow at something that won't
     be harmed
3886. Write a note in disappearing ink
3887. Learn about arches and roofs
3888. Do a gel hairstyle
3889. Dust the furniture
3890. Write cryptograms

3891. Go caroling
3892. Learn three knock-knock jokes
3893. Make a home movie of a sibling
3894. Be a reporter at large
3895. Learn a song on the piano
3896. Write a personified autobiography about something like a sneaker, clothes, hamper, car
3897. Make a big batch of Rice Krispies treats
3898. Play with Tonka trucks
3899. List ways you could earn money
3900. Sing with a band
3901. Listen to someone else's favorite music
3902. Sharpen the blunt crayons
3903. Learn about how the stock market works
3904. Throw your dog or cat a birthday party
3905. Get a roll of film and take pics of family, pets, neighborhood
3906. Take lots of photographs
3907. Teeter-totter
3908. Get a nice new collar for the dog or cat
3909. Send a thank-you note to your present teacher

3910. Do crunches
3911. Bicycle across town—or the county
3912. Read about what brought on the
      Reformation in Europe
3913. Give someone a manicure or pedicure
3914. Do isometric exercises
3915. Make a face out of peanuts and raisins
3916. Study comets and meteors
3917. Memorize the words to your favorite CD
3918. Set up a die-cast auto race down a ramp with a
      finish line
3919. Find an old bird's nest to dissect
3920. Check out a book of dinosaur crafts
3921. Find the secret of perpetual motion
3922. Discover the next Hollywood superstar
3923. Practice for an egg toss
3924. Work out
3925. Hold your breath under water
3926. Have a prehistoric party
3927. Think of a signature way of greeting people
3928. Brush your teeth

3929. Write a letter to the teacher you had last year or your old camp counselor
3930. Read something written by Benjamin Franklin
3931. Mend clothing
3932. Garden indoors or out
3933. Design furniture
3934. Pick a subject for self-instruction
3935. Work a puzzle
3936. Do a good deed
3937. Learn the art of animation
3938. Study Valley Forge and Colonial Williamsburg
3939. Hold a bake sale
3940. Inventory your room
3941. Have a dress-up, dress-down relay
3942. Collect old maps
3943. Read about Napoleon Bonaparte
3944. Work a booth at a fair
3945. Visit trailside museums
3946. Practice for the school play tryouts
3947. Read about the history of Spain and Portugal
3948. Make a pyramid replica with clay "blocks"

3949. Toast marshmallows

3950. Catch or dig your own live bait

3951. Make your own game, game board, and rules

3952. Design a cover for a compact disk or cassette tape

3953. Make a pirate ship sandwich with a cheese sail

3954. Learn the hula or mambo

3955. Make finger puppets

3956. Find out why there are nine innings in baseball

3957. Use metaphors

THINK BIG
A list of more ambitious projects and adventures

3958. Plan a trip to an astronomical observatory

3959. Carve with plaster of paris

3960. Show your animal or talent at the county fair

3961. Learn the art of field sketching

3962. Play with a velocipede

3963. Go behind the scenes of a TV show

3964. Learn a high-level computer language

3965. Ask your teacher to arrange a plant tour or two
3966. Study gestalt psychology
3967. Harvest a crop
3968. Drive a horse
3969. Try sushi
3970. Hike to another camp
3971. Watch a video on CPR and emergency first aid
3972. Go with a cousin to the movies or mall
3973. Start a rock band
3974. Learn to ride a horse
3975. "Adopt" an animal at the zoo
3976. Learn to figure-skate
3977. Watch stonemasons at work
3978. Join an archaeological dig as a volunteer
3979. Hear the muffled roar of the sea in a storm
3980. Rescue an injured animal
3981. Help send out absentee voter ballots
3982. Attend the YMCA hang-out dance
3983. Find out how they measure vitamin content
     in food
3984. Teach yourself judo or karate

5,001 Things for Kids to Do

3985. Learn a foreign language with a computer program
3986. Learn Yiddish
3987. Learn by watching workers at a construction site
3988. Watch a rocket or missile take off
3989. Work on a project looking for a cure for cancer
3990. Plunge down a water slide
3991. Examine a beaver dam
3992. Read bulletin boards at the supermarket
3993. Attend a craft fair
3994. Arrange to go on a musical field trip
3995. Arrange to visit an airport control tower
3996. Study anthropology
3997. Have a New Year's resolution party
3998. Get a tour of a big rig
3999. Do a platform dive
4000. Go traveling with a parent
4001. Break someone's serve
4002. Learn chess with a computer or computerized game

4003. Learn by watching workers at a train station

4004. Catch fish

4005. Visit a weather station

4006. Learn to clean fish

4007. Learn by osmosis

4008. Count the American flags on a five-mile walk

4009. Build a snow fort or igloo

4010. Volunteer to work at a pancake breakfast or bake sale

4011. Volunteer at the local library

4012. Write for a permit to do archaeology in your backyard

4013. Volunteer for community efforts to feed the hungry

4014. Visit a foreign restaurant and learn about the cuisine

4015. Plan a Halloween party

4016. Use the snowballs in the freezer during a summer pool party

4017. Volunteer as a scorekeeper

4018. Memorize the names of the books of the Bible

5,001 Things for Kids to Do

4019. Add words to thesaurus entries
4020. Help save a lighthouse
4021. Learn by watching workers at an airport
4022. Find out why banking hours are so short
4023. Pretend you're floating down the
        Amazon River
4024. Observe a farmer cultivating the soil
4025. Study Sanskrit
4026. Visit a war memorial
4027. Learn blueprint symbols
4028. Take a tour of a submarine
4029. Plant flowers at a school
4030. Beautify a beach
4031. Watch a farmer plowing a field
4032. Watch a road being built
4033. Walk to the deli or bakery
4034. Take a pottery course
4035. Train a bonsai tree
4036. Be a train spotter
4037. Visit a reservation
4038. Watch a play or ballet from the wings

4039. Check out the cool stuff at tag sales

4040. Go "backstage" at the grocery store

4041. Volunteer for park and rec programs

4042. Do the London *Times* acrostic

4043. Catch a fish and throw it back

4044. Play in a steel band

4045. Shop at an army-navy store

4046. Watch the *Star Wars* trilogy

4047. Watch a foreign film

4048. Make sure the outdoor pets have ID tags

4049. Ride on a roller coaster

4050. Take a sculpture course

4051. Take a pail and shovel to the beach

4052. Read *King Lear*

4053. Read a Chekov play

4054. Do sleep learning

4055. Build newspaper dowel structures

4056. Understand lungs and breathing

4057. Take ballroom dancing

4058. Listen to a fine orchestra

4059. Fool someone on April 1

4060. Understand the free enterprise system
4061. Find out why a 2x4 is not 2x4 inches
4062. Learn to use the "stacks" or shelves
     of the library
4063. Run for student government
4064. Study Native American legends about
     the constellations
4065. Investigate fast-food restaurants' use of
     environmentally safe containers
4066. Ride with a train engineer
4067. Picnic in a snowstorm
4068. Read about the formulation of natural gas
4069. Make a commitment
4070. Take underwater photos
4071. Enter a pet show
4072. Hang a light-catching mobile in a window
4073. Watch someone repair a boat
4074. Create Christmas cards on the computer
4075. Ride the pony at the grocery store
4076. Become a chess grandmaster
4077. Work at a concession stand

4078. Trick or treat for UNICEF

4079. Give anonymously to charity

4080. Ride a tractor

4081. Try maple syrup on Maypo

4082. Swing on a trapeze

4083. Read about animal senses

4084. Adventure around town

4085. Read a book on homemaking
circa 1879

4086. Recreate Aztec art

4087. Sell Girl Scout cookies

4088. Find out what kind of hen lays
extra-large eggs

4089. Create a Web page

4090. Decipher the Linear A script

4091. Scrape snow or ice off the car windows

4092. Start a notebook to record the call numbers of
often used library books

4093. Tutor younger kids

4094. Write a letter in another alphabet

4095. Measure and calculate recipes

4096. Arrange to go on a fossil dig
4097. Cultivate a close friend from a different generation
4098. Undertake a new challenge
4099. Take up piano
4100. Make "animals" out of hot dogs
4101. Set up a milk and salad bar or snack and sandwich bar
4102. Hang mistletoe
4103. Discover the next best-selling singer or music group
4104. Learn quantum physics
4105. Make a pair of leather sandals
4106. Create a mirror framed by beautiful shells
4107. Rent your favorite movie
4108. Sign up for an introductory course
4109. Go to a movie
4110. Have a carnival party
4111. Study drama
4112. Join a string quartet
4113. Watch a rainbow until it disappears

1114. Collect toy soldiers
1115. Take a walk after dinner
1116. Plan a redecorating
1117. Throw organic garbage in the yard for bugs and animals to eat
1118. Tutor disadvantaged children
1119. Read in the upper branches of a tree
1120. Milk a cow
1121. Gather neighbors to plant a community garden
1122. Get a job
1123. Build an Estes rocket
1124. Ride in a fire engine
1125. Write an essay about touring an exotic zoo
1126. Rent a tape about ancient Egypt
1127. Work with an archaeology kit
1128. Go to the county fair
1129. Volunteer at the local playhouse
1130. Learn how to play a drum
1131. Learn to cha-cha
1132. Read an old cookbook
1133. Learn to sail

4134. Volunteer at a local animal shelter
       or organization

4135. Kayak

4136. Stage a pet show at school

4137. In-line skate along a shore

4138. Visit an historical site

4139. Find out why pennies and nickels have
       smooth edges

4140. Make smoke print stationery

4141. Set up a tent in the wilderness

4142. Learn to rock climb

4143. Inflate a wading pool

4144. Find out why Saltine crackers have holes

4145. Save a turtle crossing the street

4146. Swim with a school of fish

4147. Read about indoor pollution that you cannot see

4148. Find a free translation site on the Internet

4149. Go for a shopping center stroll

4150. Devise a solution for urban blight

4151. Make friends with a camp counselor

4152. Sew moccasins from a kit

1153. Comb the high-tide line on the beach

1154. Find out the latitude and longitude of
Peoria, Illinois

1155. Care for cacti

1156. Tune a piano

1157. Read the complete works of Shakespeare

1158. Figure out what a rhetorical question is

1159. Help a photographer in a darkroom

1160. Tramp through a new country

1161. Sled down an incline

1162. Join "the regulars" at a local coffee shop

1163. Learn official secrets

1164. Write an essay about walking a history trail
and its landmarks

1165. Hold a crop walk for the Church World Service

1166. Ride on a load of hay

1167. Set up base camp

1168. Figure out which body type you are

1169. Sculpt an ice block

1170. Make a pair of puddle jumpers with tin cans

1171. Get into a lotus position

4172. Go to a petting zoo

4173. Be on a committee to get a new park installed

4174. Attend a children's theater

4175. Do exercises when sitting in a chair, airplane seat, bus, or car seat

4176. Watch a circuit board in action

4177. Take up speed skating

4178. Meet friends at the baseball field

4179. Surf the biggest waves in the area

4180. Pretend you're on a tornado chase team

4181. Do a frog stand

4182. Take a personality test

4183. Fly from a trapeze

4184. Take communion

4185. Put together a steel band

4186. Try for the lead in a theater production

4187. Hit the bowling alley

4188. Call in to a talk show

4189. Pick a difficult thing and learn it well

4190. Find frog eggs and observe the development of the life cycle

1191. Measure wind speed

1192. Play on a basketball team of the opposite sex

1193. Walk a mail route with a carrier

1194. Watch a train be switched to another track

1195. Register your dog or cat

1196. Start a pet visitation program for a local retirement
or nursing home

1197. Get elected team captain

1198. Enroll in a music education program

1199. Plan a "see the USA" trip via RV

1200. Offer to take part in market research and
try new products

1201. Be courageous in the face of difficulty
or danger

1202. Find your true calling

1203. Learn lashing

1204. Try some free-form creative problem solving

1205. Visit the post office to get a tour

1206. Inflate an air mattress

1207. Find out why hamburger bun bottoms are thin

1208. Hold an audience spellbound

5,001 Things for Kids to Do

4209. Lie on the beach

4210. Find out where flies go in the winter

4211. Form a band

4212. Study graphic design

4213. Think in front of a fire

4214. Burn the midnight oil

4215. Help wash a fire engine

4216. Visit a hall of fame

4217. Enjoy a concert on the green

4218. Help find homes for stray pets

4219. Heed the call of nature

4220. Figure out the difference between indirect and direct objects

4221. Churn your own butter

4222. Look for your great-grandparents' love letters

4223. Practice your own stunts

4224. Become active in volunteer work

4225. Raise your IQ

4226. Learn how to take good home movies

4227. Get rid of all your "unclassy" clothes

4228. Deposit gifts of money in a savings account

4229. Design a personal wardrobe

4230. Read a biology textbook

4231. Do what you can to get food to the hungry

4232. Serve the cat a kitty smorgasbord to figure out what it likes

4233. Invent the self-defrosting driveway

4234. Eat Chinese food out of the containers

4235. Start reading every book you own

4236. Hug a cow

4237. Take a military shower

4238. Help educate the public

4239. Build a campfire circle

4240. Attend a media event

4241. Buy a painting from a starving artist

4242. Support the National Wildlife Federation

4243. Visit a fresh road cut

4244. Go to a rodeo

4245. Make a friend at the lobster tank at the grocery store

4246. Make a mental map of any routes you travel

4247. Become a guide at a nature center

4248. Set your body clock

4249. Get a part-time job

4250. Review a travel destination

4251. Read the dialogues of Plato

4252. Go on safari

4253. Cut out newspaper articles about
your friends

4254. Shoot hoops at the basketball court

4255. Make a winter bouquet

4256. Browse car dealerships when they are closed

4257. Make cat treats from scratch

4258. Attend a bazaar at an ethnic church

4259. Exhibit your work at the public library

4260. Work as a volunteer at the library

4261. Make and play a shepherd pipe

4262. Identify a new astronomical phenomenon

4263. Eat what you've grown in the garden

4264. Slide down the pole in a firehouse

4265. Make a thumbnail sketch

4266. Be a tester for trampolines and pogo sticks

4267. Give a guided tour

4268. Have a fairy tale party
4269. Have an art showing
4270. Find out who collects the money
in pay phones
4271. Learn to play the accordion
4272. Go to a newspaper to see how it's made
4273. Read the original Nancy Drew mysteries
4274. Do aerial reconnaissance
4275. Do swimnastics
4276. Find out why hand dryers in bathrooms don't
have an off button
4277. Sing in the choir
4278. Try on body armor
4279. Take a bunch of tests to identify your strengths
and weaknesses
4280. Do a Chinese puzzle
4281. Cheer when the Grinch brings Christmas back
4282. Explore a junkyard
4283. Buy yourself a toy
4284. Blow up a balloon
4285. Take an aptitude test

5,001 Things for Kids to Do

4286. Learn how to use a pay phone
4287. Eat vanilla ice cream with chocolate syrup
4288. Learn by deduction
4289. Buy a pocket dictionary and thesaurus for school
4290. Sled down the little hill in the lawn
4291. Brew coffee
4292. Figure out what the different cuts of
       beef actually are
4293. Search for the end of the rainbow
4294. Sit for your portrait
4295. Venture into the wilderness
4296. Search for truth and beauty
4297. Hear the answer the trees make to the rain
       and wind
4298. Take a slicker hike in the rain
4299. Make a single-decker for little brother or sister
4300. Steal the show
4301. Take a natural history tour of the state
4302. Spelunk
4303. Commit totally to something
4304. Talk to the natives

4305. Save money for a telescope
4306. Reduce noise pollution
4307. Check out the 4-H Club exhibits at a country/county fair
4308. Sleep on a screened-in porch
4309. Show someone something new
4310. Teach someone to read
4311. Work on the school yearbook
4312. Break up watching a movie into a mini-series
4313. Arrange to go to a Saturday matinee
4314. Find out where you can hot-air balloon in your state
4315. Try to make a team
4316. Volunteer at a camp for kids with cancer
4317. Figure out when you'll be able to see a comet or shooting star
4318. Study algebra
4319. Point out constellations with a flashlight
4320. Go where you can hear the ocean pounding on the beach
4321. Create a photo op

4322. Figure out what active and passive
      is in grammar
4323. Draw on recycled paper
4324. Shout from a mountaintop
4325. Get the public schools to teach first aid, CPR, and
      the Heimlich maneuver
4326. Take the scenic route
4327. Catch a frog
4328. Visit a Civil War battlefield
4329. Take some psychological tests
4330. Study cognitive psychology
4331. Sign up for YMCA swimming lessons
4332. Decipher the language of the ancient Etruscans
4333. Eat the cookie dough
4334. Take center stage
4335. Start a college fund
4336. Watch a travelogue film
4337. Look for a gold mine
4338. Go to the beauty parlor for a treatment
      or haircut
4339. Hike a mountain range

1340. Cook over an open fire

1341. Gobble up Mom's cooking

1342. Send for an interesting back copy of a magazine

1343. Take a chance

1344. Plan to read six works of nonfiction a year

1345. Make a list of the products advertised on
        billboards and then write an essay
        about their influence

1346. Eat Doritos and Oreos together

1347. Volunteer at a Special Olympics

1348. Find out what the ice cream truck's schedule is

1349. Have a makeup and hair makeover session

1350. Watch a monster movie

1351. Sign up for a YMCA program

1352. Participate at the community center

1353. Become a Monopoly champ

1354. Do pure science

1355. Plan to study overseas for a semester

1356. Watch a news conference involving
        the president

1357. Wave to train engineers

5,001 Things for Kids to Do

4358. Take bagpipe lessons

4359. Go on a fact-finding mission

4360. Copyright a poem

4361. Visit a state park

4362. Arrange to go see a film being made

4363. Watch movies about trekking in Nepal

4364. Participate in Passover Seder

4365. Read Proust

4366. Design a retirement community

4367. Practice math by balancing a checkbook

4368. Find a lizard sleeping with one eye open

4369. Volunteer on a farm

4370. Follow baseball's spring training

4371. Start reading the hundred great books of
       Western literature

4372. Find an example of a food producer

4373. Follow a soap opera love affair

4374. Soak up some sun, with sunscreen

4375. Write a term paper

4376. Go to an audition for a movie

4377. Understand the simple machines

4378. Study comparative religion
4379. Locate the fountain of youth
4380. Scuba dive
4381. Levitate
4382. Cook risotto
4383. Find a mistake in a dictionary
4384. Knit a sweater
4385. Read a mathematics textbook
4386. Design your own . . .
4387. Solve an unsolved crime
4388. Do charcoal rubbings of gravestones
4389. Watch street theater
4390. Help build a disabled access to a building
4391. Be a daring adventurer
4392. Make a doorstop
4393. Be in a parade
4394. Try out for the band
4395. Fish, boat, or swim in the rain (if no lightning)
4396. Take a day trip to a planetarium
4397. Get soaked in a rain shower
4398. Work on a long-term project a little at a time

5,001 Things for Kids to Do

4399. Learn to read music

4400. Read *The Sayings of Confucius*

4401. Ask to meet the pilot or engineer

4402. Put flowers on a grave

4403. Take a wood carving course

4404. Design a better lunch box

4405. Look for flying saucers

4406. Go on a night hike

4407. Sail a boat

4408. Sell the most items for a fund-raiser

4409. Read about the field of advertising

4410. Visit a recording studio

4411. Feed the animals at the zoo

4412. Learn how to rewire a lamp

4413. Float around in a pool

4414. Learn to interpret character from the shape of
the head

4415. Attend a benefit concert

4416. Capture data

4417. Be a hero to someone

4418. End world hunger

1419. Find something wild you can eat
1420. Put a flower in the locker of a person you like
1421. Ride with a postal carrier for a day
1422. Experiment
1423. Make sure your parents vote
1424. Become an expert with a Swiss Army knife
1425. Be in the town Fourth of July parade
1426. Locate some natural cast-off (leaf, feather, seed . . .)
1427. Make friends with an elderly neighbor
1428. Have a water race
1429. Visit a chocolate factory
1430. Go on a retreat
1431. Take a nature-writing course
1432. Poke holes in a box and use shoelaces to play telephone operator
1433. Finish a riveting book
1434. Order a vegetarian meal
1435. Break camp
1436. Take care of younger children when you are watching a sports event

5,001 Things for Kids to Do

4437. Cavort on the first day of spring
4438. Savor the calm after the storm
4439. Take an IQ test
4440. Invent a liquid face-lift
4441. Be a water-leak detective
4442. Browse antiques shops
4443. Watch a closed-circuit TV broadcast
4444. Cook a Cajun dish
4445. Get school credit for volunteer work
4446. Take sports lessons given by the park and recreation department
4447. Learn to handle a handsaw and a hammer
4448. Go to the dentist without a struggle
4449. Take pottery lessons
4450. Improve your archery
4451. Do yogic breathing
4452. Check out biofeedback
4453. Do something to help stop acid rain
4454. Publish an article
4455. Watch *Sesame Street*
4456. Learn to swan dive

1457. Find a cure for heart disease

1458. Try everything once

1459. Sign up at a dance studio

1460. Walk to or from school with someone

1461. Slide on the ice without falling

1462. Spend the day at a railway or bus station people-watching

1463. Take up woodworking

1464. Find out why Jack is a nickname for John

1465. Sit in on an introductory lesson on something you're interested in

1466. Give the cat some hairball medicine

1467. Enter a hog-calling contest

1468. Watch skating at the ice rink

1469. Create a bag of tricks

1470. Throw a soda fountain party with a theme

1471. Organize a supermarket food drive

1472. Ask for the recipe of anything you really enjoy

1473. Darn any socks with holes

1474. Bike to school

1475. Read all the books you've been saving up

4476. Bid at an auction
4477. Apply for a spot on a space shuttle or
      space station
4478. Play the piano without complaining
4479. Be a caddy
4480. Be the first to fight for a just cause
4481. Volunteer at a hospital
4482. Build a snow family
4483. Find a chemical reaction going on
4484. Fix a snack to share with a sibling
4485. Be the first customer at a sale
4486. Walk aimlessly
4487. Plant a tree on your birthday
4488. Learn the Chicken Scratch code
4489. Get a Mexican jumping bean to jump
      500,000 times
4490. Start a lonely hearts club
4491. Push a tire like a hoop
4492. Give a gift anonymously
4493. Find a cure for an addiction
4494. Figure out where *apple pie order* originated

4495. Plan how you can start collecting books

4496. Comprehend the theory of relativity

4497. Serve someone chicken soup when they are sick

4498. Try a new toothpaste

4499. Find out why humans evolved into losing most of their bodily hair

4500. Seek an apprenticeship or mentor

4501. Campaign to outlaw handguns

4502. Watch a friend's piano recital

4503. Plant a shrub

4504. Try to earn a blue ribbon

4505. Have a tiny and giant party

4506. Operate a ham radio

4507. Help save the area's wetlands

4508. Take a day trip to a science museum

4509. Recycle your old crayons

4510. Choose a campsite

4511. Enroll in a research program

4512. Find out why shoes aren't laced in the store or when they are delivered

4513. Eat at a pizza parlor

5,001 Things for Kids to Do

4514. Choose a Christmas craft project

4515. Take a sibling out for a pizza slice

4516. Start a double Dutch contest

4517. Do a flip turn in swimming

4518. Take a walk just as it is turning dark

4519. Drop beans straight down into a tin can

4520. See a movie without reading the review

4521. Learn needlepoint

4522. In the fall, plant tulips

4523. Join a youth club

4524. Plan to host a foreign exchange student

4525. Read *Cricket* magazine

4526. Figure out how to boil pasta without
it foaming

4527. Learn ancient Greek

4528. Try out a new recipe with a parent

4529. Improve your communications skills

4530. Make tunnels in the beach sand

4531. Read books on getting organized

4532. Visit a quarry

4533. Arrange for a bonfire night

1534. Collect old *National Geographic* magazines

1535. Be the first person anywhere to do something

1536. Hit the golf links

1537. Hire a limo to take Mom and Dad out
      for the night

1538. Learn the rule for doubling consonants

1539. Go to a fancy restaurant and buy a dessert

1540. Learn to type 80 wpm

1541. Take a course in public speaking

1542. Apply for a scholarship

1543. Learn piano by computer

1544. Cure a phobia

1545. Make a sand castle shaped like the stone city
      Great Zimbabwe

1546. Get all the lumps out of the mashed potatoes

1547. Celebrate the holidays of all the religions

1548. Ride a pack animal

1549. Learn a trade

1550. Find a cure for the common cold

1551. Jog along a waterfront

1552. Invent a low-calorie dessert

4553. Do not say a word all day

4554. Consult a fortune-teller

4555. Go on patrol with cops on the beat

4556. Learn something about practical politics;
understand how political power is used

4557. Walk four miles to get a really big breakfast

4558. Take the Red Cross first-aid course

4559. Submit a suggestion that saves a
company money

4560. Visit a printer to see the printing process

4561. Go to a jazz festival

4562. Do pink cloud relaxation

4563. Make a breakthrough scientific discovery

4564. Anticipate someone's every need

4565. Spend a day alone in the woods, thinking

4566. Lobby for and against causes

4567. Read *The Odyssey*

4568. Make a pot of coffee or tea

4569. Buy vegetables from a farmer's truck

4570. Volunteer time for a community event

4571. Learn to use Usenet on the Web

1572. Nap in a field of wildflowers

1573. Write to a pen pal in a foreign country

1574. Send a thank-you to a great camp counselor

1575. Try to win a week's vacation

1576. Help a neighborhood watch group

1577. Look for imprints in the snow and identify them

1578. Send CARE packages anonymously

1579. Read about trade and industry

1580. Put on old clothes and stand outside in the rain

1581. Attract birds to the yard

1582. Donate money to a hunger project

1583. Meet your favorite radio personality

1584. Volunteer at a hospice

1585. Toboggan

1586. Build a shelter

1587. Give yourself a year and read a dictionary
       cover to cover

1588. Get a beauty makeover at a department store

1589. Watch a black-and-white movie

1590. Listen to rain on the roof

1591. Have an astrologer cast your chart

5,001 Things for Kids to Do

4592. Contribute to conservation efforts
4593. Read about a religion you know nothing about
4594. Wish on a falling star
4595. Tour your state capitol building
4596. Weave a room with yarn, string, or ribbon
4597. Make a checkerboard
4598. Build with cards
4599. Make a "pinball" machine out of cardboard, bobby pins, and small balls
4600. Develop and lift fingerprints
4601. Make ball hand puppets out of tennis balls
4602. Make a tent inside
4603. Make a wig of yarn
4604. Weave a God's eye
4605. Make a paper cup sculpture with clothespins, staples, or paper clips
4606. Do straw and clip building
4607. Perfect a balloon rocket
4608. Do picture printing
4609. Make noodle jewelry and button rings
4610. Create iron-ons with crayon drawings

4611. Make a squeeze painting in a plastic bag

4612. Make lunch without cooking

4613. Build a three-stick stool

4614. Float a paddle-block boat

4615. Make a hammock from seventy-five six-pack carriers

4616. Build an icosahedron dome

4617. Construct a musical nails instrument

4618. Make a wave machine in a bottle

4619. Make shoes out of tire treads

4620. Make soft play boomerangs

4621. Create a water slide

4622. Make a button yo-yo

4623. Do a dot-and-triangle pencil game

Self-Improvement To-Do List

4624. Drink eight glasses of water every day

4625. Find inner peace

4626. Learn to listen

4627. Ask for help

4628. Eat moderately

5,001 Things for Kids to Do

4629. Have a positive effect on people

4630. Meet someone halfway

4631. Respect your elders

4632. Throw away your old security blanket

4633. Swing for the fence

4634. Look out for someone

4635. Be cool

4636. Go to bed if you are tired

4637. Learn patience

4638. Perfect your table manners

4639. Strive for excellence, not perfection

4640. Stand up for your principles

4641. Tell the truth

4642. Get rid of excess baggage

4643. Compromise

4644. Count your blessings

4645. Admit your mistakes

4646. Calculate the consequences of an action before
       you act

4647. Give someone a pat on the back

4648. Reinvent yourself

4649. Relive your fondest memory
4650. Acknowledge your weaknesses
4651. Ask many questions
4652. Be an early bird
4653. Improve your grammar
4654. Lose your insecurities
4655. Enjoy the little things in life
4656. Listen to your inner voice
4657. Make life your classroom
4658. Tackle a problem
4659. Practice self-control
4660. Give up your bad habits
4661. Practice tolerance
4662. Celebrate joy
4663. Do everything to the best of your ability
4664. Watch less TV
4665. Take the road less traveled
4666. Overcome shyness or aggressiveness
4667. Be aware of grammar when you write
4668. Try to be a leader
4669. Eat all your spinach

4670. Do not put off till tomorrow what you
can do today
4671. Mend fences
4672. Do extra-credit schoolwork
4673. Act your age
4674. Do your homework and know your facts
4675. Abstain from bad behavior
4676. Be a role model for a younger person
4677. Study hard
4678. Lend a hand
4679. Meet all your deadlines
4680. Exceed people's expectations
4681. Limit your telephone calls to two minutes
4682. Keep on learning new things
4683. Offer positive reinforcement
4684. Make up your mind

You Can Play . . .

4685. Alleyway
4686. Alphabet charades (spell with your body)

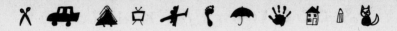

4687. Alphabet game—finding something that starts with A-to-Z

4688. Amnesia (identity taped on back)

4689. Animal, vegetable, or mineral

4690. Army

4691. Ashte kashte

4692. Association chain

4693. Associations

4694. Balloon volleyball

4695. Balloonminton

4696. Barnyard peanut hunt

4697. Baseball pickle

4698. Basketball 21, 25, or 31

4699. Basketball around the world

4700. Basketball horse

4701. Basketball shootout

4702. Beach volleyball

4703. Bean bag archery

4704. Beanbag toss

4705. Beauty parlor

4706. Bilbo catcher

4707. Blind judgment

4708. Blind man's bluff

4709. Blind man's stick

4710. Blind man's treasure hunt

4711. Blind postman

4712. Blindfold obstacle walk

4713. Blow volleyball

4714. Board games

4715. Botticelli

4716. Brooklyn Bridge

4717. Broom hockey

4718. Broomball

4719. Bump, set, personal

4720. Buzz, fizz, or buzz-fizz

4721. Captain, may I?

4722. Catch

4723. Categories

4724. Category charades

4725. Checkers with the computer

4726. Chinese checkers

4727. Chinese rebels

4728. Circle dodge ball
4729. Circle golf
4730. Clue
4731. Coffeepot
4732. Coin throwing game
4733. Compass relay or compass treasure hunt
4734. Computer game
4735. Conkers
4736. Conquest
4737. Consequences
4738. Cootie
4739. Cops and robbers
4740. Crab relay
4741. Cranium
4742. Croquet
4743. Crossover dodge ball
4744. Danish rounders
4745. Darts
4746. Do this, do that
4747. Dodgeball
4748. Dog and bone

4749. Dog patch olympics
4750. Dog sports
4751. Doom and all its sequels
4752. Drop dead dice
4753. Drop the handkerchief
4754. Duck, duck, goose
4755. Electronic football
4756. Elephant's tail
4757. Farmer in the dell
4758. Fighting serpents
4759. Firefighter's race
4760. Fivestones
4761. Flashlight tag
4762. Floor hockey
4763. Follow the leader
4764. Four square
4765. Fox and geese
4766. Freeze tag
4767. Game of graces
4768. Go
4769. Golf scramble

4770. Golf skins
4771. Gossip relay
4772. Halma
4773. Hangman
4774. Heroes and villains
4775. Hex
4776. Hide-and-seek
4777. Hockey baseball
4778. Hopscotch
4779. Horseshoes
4780. Hot and cold
4781. Hot potato
4782. House
4783. Hyena chase
4784. I spy
4785. I went on a trip
4786. Play in the sandbox
4787. Play indoor games
4788. Jack and Jill
4789. Jacob's Ladder
4790. Jacks

4791. Jailer
4792. Kalah
4793. Kangaroo relay
4794. Kick the can
4795. Kickball
4796. King of the hill
4797. Labyrinth
4798. Lasca
4799. Lawn bowls
4800. Legs-crossed relay
4801. Life
4802. London Bridge
4803. Ludo
4804. Magazine scavenger hunt
4805. Mah jongg
4806. Man in the street
4807. Mancala games
4808. Marble sharpshooter
4809. Marco Polo
4810. Miniature golf
4811. Monkey in the middle

4812. Monopoly

4813. Mother, may I?

4814. Murals

4815. Murder in the dark

4816. Museum scavenger hunt

4817. Musical chairs

4818. Myst and Riven until they are solved

4819. Name that tune

4820. Nelson's eye

4821. New game

4822. Nine men's morris

4823. Ninepins

4824. Number associations

4825. Nyout

4826. Observation, a guessing game

4827. Obstacle golf

4828. Old maid

4829. One minute please

4830. One-foot relay

4831. Ownership musical chairs

4832. Pachisi

4833. Paddleball
4834. Parcheesi
4835. Parent
4836. Party game telephone
4837. Peekaboo
4838. Pegboard solitaire
4839. Penny ante
4840. Pepper
4841. Pewter coin whirligig
4842. Pick-up basketball
4843. Pick-up sticks
4844. Pictionary
4845. Piggyback race
4846. Pirate
4847. Pokémon
4848. Pom pom pull away
4849. Post office
4850. Potato relay
4851. Progressive games
4852. Proverb charades
4853. Proverbs

4854. Queen's guard
4855. Radio station
4856. Red rover
4857. Reversi
4858. Ring toss
4859. Ringo
4860. Risk
4861. Rock, scissors, paper
4862. Rolling hoop
4863. Roulette
4864. Sack relay
4865. Salta
4866. Sap tim pun
4867. Sardines
4868. Scrabble
4869. Seven-up
4870. Sharks and minnows
4871. Shogi
4872. Shooting around (harvey ball)
4873. Shove soccer
4874. Shovelboard

4875. Sidewalk golf
4876. Simon says
4877. Skittles (soccer bowling)
4878. Snooker
4879. Soccer baseball
4880. Soccer croquet
4881. Soccer golf
4882. Soccer hockey
4883. Soccer tennis
4884. Soccer volleyball
4885. Spellicans
4886. Spoken charades
4887. Spud
4888. Squails
4889. Square tic-tac-toe
4890. Squeak piggy squeak
4891. Statues
4892. Steal the dribble
4893. Stickball
4894. Stop the music
4895. Street hockey

4896. Suitcase relay
4897. Sweet tooth
4898. Tabletop ninepins
4899. Taboo
4900. Ankle tag
4901. Ball tag
4902. Piggyback tag
4903. Prayer tag
4904. Skunk tag
4905. Target golf
4906. Teakettle
4907. Ten step buff
4908. Tennis baseball
4909. Tennis match
4910. Tetherball
4911. The make me laugh game
4912. Thieves
4913. Three-legged race
4914. Tic-tac-toe
4915. Tiddlywinks
4916. Touch football

5,001 Things for Kids to Do

4917. Traveler's alphabet
4918. Triangular tug-of-war
4919. Trouble
4920. TV station
4921. Play along with a TV game show and keep score
4922. Twenty questions
4923. Twister
4924. Two square
4925. Wall ball
4926. What's in my hand? guessing game
4927. Wheelbarrow race
4928. Who am I?
4929. Wiffle ball
4930. Wood whirligig
4931. Word association game or make mind maps
4932. World championship chess
4933. Yahtzee

Card Games

1934. All fives
1935. Auction pitch
1936. Bezique
1937. Boston
1938. Bridge
1939. Calabrasella
1940. Canasta
1941. Casino
1942. Crazy eights
1943. Cribbage
1944. Ecarte
1945. Euchre
1946. Fish/go fish
1947. Five hundred
1948. Forty-five
1949. Gin or gin rummy
1950. Grand
1951. Hearts

4952. Imperial
4953. Knaves
4954. Loo
4955. Michigan rummy
4956. Napoleon
4957. Oh hell
4958. Pinochle
4959. Piquet
4960. Pope Joan
4961. Preference
4962. Beggar my neighbor
4963. Card dominoes
4964. Cheat
4965. Concentration
4966. Donkey
4967. Give away
4968. Go boom
4969. Knockout whist
4970. Linger longer
4971. Menagerie
4972. Racing demon

1973. Rolling stone
1974. Sequence
1975. Slapjack
1976. Snap
1977. Spit
1978. Stealing bundles
1979. War

Solitaire

1980. Accordion
1981. Bristol
1982. Calculation
1983. Canfield
1984. Clock
1985. Crazy quilt
1986. Eight away
1987. Florentine
1988. Flower garden
1989. Friday the 13th
1990. Frog

5,001 Things for Kids to Do

4991. King Albert
4992. Klondike
4993. Leapfrog
4994. Maze
4995. Miss Milligan
4996. Monte Carlo
4997. Poker
4998. Pyramid
4999. Russian
5000. Scorpion
5001. Spider

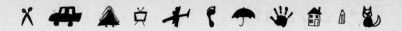

Supply List

Absorbent cotton

Acorns

Aluminum foil

Balloons

Band-Aids

Beads

Birthday cake ornaments

Bobby pins

Bottle caps

Bows

Boxes

Business cards

Buttons

Candy wrappers

Caps from soda and water bottles

Cardboard boxes and tubes

5,001 Things for Kids to Do

Cardboard milk cartons
Carpet scraps
Cereals and grains
Chalk
Clay
Clear glue
Cloth scraps
Clothespins
Coat hangers
Coins
Colored pencils
Comic strips
Confetti
Construction paper
Corks
Cotton swabs
Coverall
Craft or popsicle sticks
Crayons
Crepe paper
Doilies

Dried beans
Dried leaves
Drinking straws
Egg cartons
Egg shells
Empty spools
Fabric scraps
Feathers
Felt-tip pens
Flowers
Foil hearts and stars
Food labels
Food trays and baskets
Glitter
Glue stick
Graph paper
Hairpins
Ice cream sticks
Index cards
Jar lids
Junk mail and catalogs

Keys
Leaves
Library paste
Magazines
Maps
Markers
Nails
Non-toxic glues or glue sticks
Nuts
Nuts, bolts, and screws
Old bedsheets
Old newspapers
Old shoelaces
Old socks and stockings
Old toothbrushes
Paints and paintbrushes
Paint sample cards
Paper, colored and plain
Paper bags
Paper clips
Paper hole reinforcements

Paper napkins and towels
Paper plates and cups
Paper towel and toilet paper tubes
Parcel paper
Pasta
Pebbles
Pencils
Pens
Picture frames
Pipe cleaners
Plastic containers and tops
Plastic flowers
Play money
Pocket mirrors
Popsicle sticks
Postage stamps (used)
Postcards
Poster board
"Reject" photographs
Ribbon
Rubber bands

5,001 Things for Kids to Do

Rubber stamps
Ruler
Safety scissors
Sand
Scrap paper
Screws
Seashells
Seeds
Sequins
Sheet music
Shirt cardboard
Snapshots
Soda can tops
Sponges
Sports emblems
Stapler
Sticks
Stickers
Stones and pebbles
String
Styrofoam

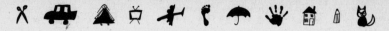

Thread
Ticket stubs
Tin cans
Tinsel
Tissue paper
Toothpicks
Twigs
Twist ties
Used gift wrap and ribbon
Wallpaper scraps
Washable markers
Washers
Watercolor paints
White glue
Wire
Wrapping paper
Yarn

℗ PLUME

PARENTING STRATEGIES

DISCIPLINE THAT WORKS *Promoting Self-Discipline in Children*—**Dr. Thomas Gordon** In this insightful book, Dr. Thomas Gordon, founder of P.E.T. (Parent Effectiveness Training) and an acclaimed clinical psychologist, provides an important new strategy to help adults empower children to become self-reliant, make positive decisions, and control their own behavior.

0-452-26643-2

CHILDREN: THE CHALLENGE *The Classic Work on Improving Parent-Child Relations—Intelligent, Human, and Eminently Practical*—**Rudolf Dreikurs, M.D., with Vicki Soltz, R.N.** Based on a lifetime of experience with children, Dr. Rudolf Dreikurs, one of America's foremost child psychiatrists, presents a step-by-step program that teaches parents how to cope with the common problems that occur during a child's growth—from toddler through preteen years.

0-452-26655-6

PARENTING AND ATTENTION DEFICIT DISORDER

THE ATTENTION DEFICIT ANSWER BOOK *The Best Medications and Parenting Strategies for Your Child*—**Alan Wachtel, M.D., with Michael Boyette** Taking the latest medical findings and presenting them in an easy-to-follow format, Dr. Alan Wachtel, Clinical Associate Professor of Psychiatry at the New York University School of Medicine, offers a program combining medical treatment with nondrug therapies that is tailored to each individual child's needs.

0-452-27941-0

THE MYTH OF THE A.D.D. CHILD *50 Ways to Improve Your Child's Behavior and Attention Span Without Drugs, Labels, or Coercion*—**Thomas Armstrong, Ph.D.** In this essential guide for both parents and professionals, Dr. Armstrong offers fifty nondrug strategies for helping a child overcome attention and behavioral problems by focusing on the root causes of these problems.

0-452-27547-4

℗ PLUME

TIMELY TOPICS IN PARENTING

THE TAO OF PARENTING *The Ageless Wisdom of Taoism and the Art of Raising Children*—**Greta Nagel, Ph.D.** Dr. Greta Nagel brings the way of the Tao to contemporary families by showing how to apply its timeless wisdom to each phase of a child's life, and by demonstrating an approach to parenting that suits individual needs.

0-452-28005-2

THE FAMILY VIRTUES GUIDE *Simple Ways to Bring Out the Best in Our Children and Ourselves*—**Linda Kavelin Popov** *The Family Virtues Guide* is a multicultural, interfaith handbook showing parents and teachers how to turn words into actions and ideals into realities.

0-452-27810-4

Visa and Mastercard holders can order Plume books by calling
1-800-253-6476.
They are also available at your local bookstore. Allow 4–6 weeks for delivery.
This offer is subject to change without notice.